DAVID & CHARLES SOURCES FOR
CONTEMPORARY ISSUES SERIES

PRIVACY

D0869105

SERIES EDITOR: *Ben Whitaker*

published

ANGLO-AMERICAN RELATIONS SINCE THE SECOND WORLD WAR
Ian S. McDonald

BRITISH BROADCASTING
Anthony Smith

THE BRITISH PRESS
Anthony Smith

EASTERN EUROPE SINCE STALIN
Jonathan Steele

THE POPULATION PROBLEM
Stanley Johnson

TRADE UNIONS IN GREAT BRITAIN
John Hughes and Harold Pollins

in preparation

CHILDREN IN SOCIETY
Rosalind Brook

CIVIL RIGHTS
Tom Harper

THE CIVIL SERVICE
Maurice Kogan and David Shapiro

COMMUNITY ACTION
Peter Marris and Cynthia Cockburn

THE CONTROL OF THE CITY
David C. Thorns

THE ELECTORAL SYSTEM
David Butler

HIGHER EDUCATION
Brian MacArthur

LOCAL GOVERNMENT
Owen A. Hartley

POVERTY
Frank Field

REVOLUTION
Adam Roberts

SOUTH AFRICA
Sir Robert Birley

THE WELFARE STATE
Geoffrey Smith and E. T. Ashton

WESTERN EUROPEAN INTEGRATION
Malcolm Crawford

DAVID & CHARLES SOURCES FOR CONTEMPORARY ISSUES SERIES

PRIVACY

Compiled and Edited by

Mervyn Jones

DAVID & CHARLES

NEWTON ABBOT   LONDON   NORTH POMFRET (VT)   VANCOUVER

0 7153 6519 3

Set in 11 on 13pt Baskerville and printed in
Great Britain by Latimer Trend & Company Ltd
for David & Charles (Holdings) Limited
South Devon House Newton Abbot Devon

Published in the United States of America
by David & Charles Inc North Pomfret
Vermont 05053 USA

Published in Canada by Douglas David & Charles Limited
3645 McKechnie Drive West Vancouver BC

Contents

		PAGE
INTRODUCTION		11
	PART ONE: THE NEW TECHNOLOGY	26
	TECHNIQUES OF INTRUSION	26
1	Alan F. Westin. *Technological devices*	27
2	R. V. Jones. *The 'harmonica bug'*	32
3	Louis B. Sohn. *Mini transmitters*	33
4	Stanley M. Beck. *Mini recorders*	33
5	Younger Report. *Comprehensive list of surveillance devices*	34
6	Donald Madgwick. *Police use of bugging devices*	37
7	Alan F. Westin. *Bugging devices on sale in the USA*	38
8	UN Report. *Use of bugging devices in the Netherlands*	39
9	Donald Madgwick. *Bugging devices for sale in Britain*	39
10	Younger Report. *Devices available in Britain*	40
	UNDER ASSESSMENT	41
11	Arthur R. Miller. *Personality tests*	41
12	Alan F. Westin. *Personality tests*	44
13	Director-General, ILO. *Prejudicial results of tests*	46
14	Alan F. Westin. *A test taker's right to privacy*	47
15A	UN Report. *Reactive assessment*	49
15B	UN Report. *Non-reactive assessment*	50

THE COMPUTER REVOLUTION   52
16A   Alan F. Westin. *Probes and dossiers in the USA*   53
16B   Alan F. Westin. *Master files of individual lives*   54
17   UN Report. *Magnetic card files*   56
18   Arthur R. Miller. *Pen registers*   57
19   Younger Report. *Number of computers in the UK*   57
20   Justice Report. *Range of computerised information*   58
21   Alan F. Westin. *Data banks*   60
22   Justice Report. *Data banks*   61
23   Sawyer and Schechter. *Data centres*   62
24   NCCL conference. *Access to computer information*   63
25   Arthur R. Miller. *Damaging and distorted information*   65
26A   NCCL conference. *Storage and interpretation of psychi-
      atric data*   68
26B   NCCL conference. *Storing medical histories*   71
27   Harvey Matusow. *The computer's inability to recognise
      mistakes*   74
28   NCCL conference. *Computer security systems*   75
29A   Younger Report. *Security safeguards for computerised
      information*   77
29B   Younger Report. *Recommendations on computer procedure*   78
30   British Computer Society. *Lack of reliability in com-
      puter service*   81
31   UN Report. *Control of access to data bank information*   82

PART TWO: THE POWER OF THE STATE   84
POLICE RECORDS   84
32   Assistant Chief Constable, Devon and Cornwall
      Constabulary. *Reply to a petition of protest*   85
33A   James B. Rule. *Criminal Records Office filing system*   86
33B   James B. Rule. *Police use of CRO information*   90
33C   James B. Rule. *Computerisation of police records*   93

WATCHDOGS OF LOYALTY   95
34A   CLSPP. *State security risks*   97
34B   CLSPP. *Employment restrictions*   99

34C CLSPP. *Security check* 104

PUBLIC SERVANTS AND PRIVATE PEOPLE 105
35A NCCL. *Information obtained from official surveys* 106
35B NCCL. *Staines Housing Department's files* 107
36 DHSS. *Cohabitation* 108
37A Ruth Lister. *Cohabitation and the 'AX' code* 110
37B Ruth Lister. *Individual cases investigated* 111
37C Ruth Lister. *Investigators at work* 115
37D Ruth Lister. *Tribunal hearings of cohabitation cases* 118

PART THREE: EXPOSED POSITIONS 122
THE MASS MEDIA 122
38 Mervyn Jones. *Reporters and the public* 122
39A 'Twentieth Century'. *Interview with Brigitte Bardot* 126
39B 'Twentieth Century'. *The public image* 127
40A Younger Report. *Newspaper publicity* 128
40B Younger Report. *The Press Council* 132
40C Younger Report. *Use of recording techniques* 132
40D Younger Report. *Responsibilities of broadcasting authorities* 134

PRIVATE EYES 134
41 NCCL. *Intrusion by private detectives* 134
42A Peter Harvey. *A private investigation experiment* 137
42B Peter Harvey. *Exposure of a public mischief* 140
43A Younger Report. *Private investigators* 141
43B Younger Report. *Reprehensible practices* 143

THE BANKS 145
44A Younger Report. *Information supplied by banks* 145
44B Younger Report. *Customers' credits and bankers' references* 146

CREDIT AND DEBT 149
45A Younger Report. *Credit rating agencies* 150

45B Younger Report. *Control of Information bill*   155
46   NCCL. *Debt collecting procedures*   156
47   Younger Report. *Debt collecting procedures*   158

GETTING A JOB   159
48   Younger Report. *Information requested by prospective
     employers*   160
49   James B. Rule. *Criminal records of employees*   162
     STUDENTS AND PRIVACY   164
50   Younger Report. *Statistical record of students*   164
51   'The Guardian'. *University of East Anglia's student
     documents*   166
52A Warwick University files. *Report of a Labour Party
     meeting*   167
52B Warwick University files. *Letter to the Chairman of
     the Warwickshire Education Committee*   168
52C Warwick University files. *Minutes of meeting of Officers
     of Council*   169
52D Warwick University files. *Letter from the Headmaster
     of William Ellis School*   170
52E Warwick University files. *Letter to the Headmaster of
     William Ellis School*   171

PART FOUR: REMEDIES   172
THE PRIVACY DEBATE   172
53A Brian Walden MP. *Privacy Bill debate*   172
53B Eric Heffer MP. *Privacy Bill debate*   176
53C James Callaghan, Home Secretary. *Privacy Bill
     debate*   178
54A Robert Carr, Home Secretary. *Debate on Younger
     Report*   181
54B Shirley Williams MP. *Debate on Younger Report*   187
54C Maurice Edelman MP. *Debate on Younger Report*   188
54D Timothy Raison MP. *Debate on Younger Report*   190
54E R. C. Mitchell MP. *Debate on Younger Report*   193
54F Ted Leadbitter MP. *Debate on Younger Report*   195

A RIGHT OF PRIVACY   196
55   Justice Report. *No legal remedy*   197
56A Younger Report. *Legal convictions*   199
56B Younger Report. *Recommended legislation*   200
57A Brandeis and Warren. *The case for a right to privacy*   201
57B Brandeis and Warren. *Law of defamation*   203
58   Brian Walden MP. *Privacy Bill*   206
59A Younger Report. *Committee's conclusions on legislation*   211
59B Alexander Lyon MP. *Minority report on legislation*   216

SUGGESTIONS FOR FURTHER READING   221

ACKNOWLEDGEMENTS   223

INDEX   225

B

X

Introduction

On 26 November 1969 Mr Brian Walden, MP, introduced in the House of Commons a bill 'to establish a right of privacy, to make consequential amendments to the law of evidence, and for connected purposes'. Two similar bills had been presented during the decade, one in the House of Lords in 1961 and one in the Commons in 1967. Private members' bills, in modern parliamentary conditions, do not get anywhere unless they are favoured and assisted by the Government; the movers were well aware of this, and their aim was to get the Government thinking—and, if possible, acting—on a matter which had become a subject of increasing concern. Whether Mr Walden's forceful speech made an impression, or whether it was a case of third time lucky, this aim was at least partly achieved. The Government reacted by setting up a Committee on Privacy, with these terms of reference: 'To consider whether legislation is needed to give further protection to the individual citizen and to commercial and industrial interests against intrusions into privacy by private persons and organisations, or by companies, and to make recommendations.'

Setting up a committee can be regarded, as one pleases, either as an earnest effort to secure full and cool consideration of a complex subject, or as a delaying device to fend off pressure for action on a tricky issue. In this case, it was probably a bit of both. Privacy certainly is a complex question, as we shall see in these pages, and solutions which appear obvious at first glance turn out to have snags when their possible consequences are examined. It is also true that vocal sections of opinion and powerful interests were bound to be angered by the kind of proposals that Mr Walden was urging. From the point of view of authority, the best imaginable result would be for the Committee to report that privacy was indeed a serious matter, but that threats to it were exaggerated by the anxious and that existing laws gave adequate protection. In the composition of the Committee, at all events, the Government played fair. The chairman was Sir Kenneth Younger, a former minister retired from politics; the members included Mr Alexander Lyon, MP, who had introduced the 1967 Privacy Bill, and a number of people whose views on the question were not yet known and perhaps not yet formulated in their own minds. It was undoubtedly a thoughtful and objective inquiry—so far as such a thing is possible in human affairs. The Committee was appointed on 13 May 1970 and reported on 25 May 1972. The Younger Report will be extensively quoted and discussed in this book, for it is the most wide-ranging and up-to-date investigation of the subject of privacy in Britain.

But before we make up our own minds as to whether—and how—privacy is threatened, and how it should be protected, we have to be clear what we mean by it. We can start with a simple definition: 'the right to be let alone'. This was the sound, straightforward phrase coined by Judge Cooley in 1888; he used it, in fact, as a chapter heading in his authoritative book on torts. The Younger Report found the definition to be less than helpful, commenting: 'An unqualified right of this kind would in any event be an unrealistic concept, incompatible with the concept of society'. This comment demonstrates at the outset why privacy is a tricky subject and why we need to think hard about it. However, the key word in the sentence just quoted is 'unqualified'; we can be pretty sure that neither Judge Cooley, nor anyone else except perhaps a hermit, has ever considered 'the right to be let alone'—or indeed the desire to be let alone—as an absolute. The fact remains that the words strike a chord. 'The right to be let alone' is what most people mean by privacy. And most people feel that they have, or ought to have, such a right, however much they would be willing to see it qualified or limited in various respects.

Next, it is worth asking why there is concern about privacy —and about threats to privacy—in countries like Britain, the nations of western Europe, and the United States of America; that is, in industrialised nations, developed nations, nations that have attracted such labels as 'the affluent society' and 'the admass society'. The Younger Committee pondered on this question, and pointed out that in certain respects people in a preindustrial society enjoyed (and enjoy, for there are still plenty of such societies) less privacy than we do. There are no 'keep out' notices in a village where everyone works on the land or in such craft workshops as the blacksmith's forge or the bakery. A community of this kind is like a family, with the family habits of aid in time of trouble and disapproval of behaviour that transgresses accepted standards. (Often, since everyone is more or less related, it is literally a big family.) Anyone who is lazy, or dirty, or a drunkard has very little chance of keeping it quiet, nor indeed of being let alone. Courtships and marriages, pregnancies and births, illnesses and deaths are public events. The peasant village—or the Scottish clan before 1745, or the African tribe—is by its nature a society in which everything is everybody's business. People with such a background accept quite readily (for instance, in a Chinese commune) infringements of privacy that seem appalling to modern Western man. Indeed, preindustrial groups drawn into the industrial world—Welsh mining villages are a good example—clung as long as they could to the old customs and traditions, whose gradual disappearance is generally considered to be a loss despite the gain in privacy.

In this perspective, the Younger Report is justified in saying:

The modern middle-class family of two parents and their children, relatively sound-proofed in their semi-detached house, relatively unseen behind their privet hedge and rose trellis, travelling with determined reserve on public transport or insulated in the family car, shopping in the super-market and entertained by television, are probably more private in the sense of being unnoticed in all their everyday doings than any sizeable section of the population in any other time or place.

However, to draw this contrast in simple terms of more privacy or less privacy is to omit a vital element—that of *consent* to what may be called exposure. To the degree that the old-style community is like a family, the rule of 'everything is everybody's business' is accepted, or seen as natural, in the same way as in a family. (I am not forgetting that demands for privacy are made, often with great emotional force, in the family too; but this shows that family relationships have changed in the modern world along the same lines as other social relationships). In the traditional way of living, privacy was sacrificed only within the community—that is, it was surrendered to people who were individually known and who shared the communal outlook and standards. Moreover, the surrender was a two-way traffic; what John knew about Thomas, Thomas also knew about John. This ruled out the possibility of being judged and condemned by someone who was perhaps guilty of the same transgression as oneself but was successfully concealing it. The intrusion and exposure that did not have to be feared was intrusion by, and exposure to, strangers. No one was filmed for television while shopping, or asked where he was going by an official taking a traffic survey, or interviewed by a sociologist, or cross-examined about her private life by a clerk of the Supplementary Benefits Commission.

It is in relation to authority that this point can be made most sharply. A striking episode in Richard Llewellyn's *How Green was My Valley*, a novel set in the Rhondda in the nineteenth century, describes the shock caused by the first appearance (in exceptionally grave circumstances) of police from outside the valley. There were, in fact, no police in the valley, offences being curbed by paternal authority over the young and by community action. Nowadays, of course, it is a common experience to be questioned or reprimanded by a policeman—often a policeman in a patrol car whom one has never seen before and is unlikely ever to see again.

The whole question of privacy, indeed, is connected with that of the increasingly impersonal nature of authority. It can be argued—it certainly would be argued by an official Committee on Freedom—that modern man enjoys a degree of freedom unknown to his ancestors. His rights are protected by a complex structure of elected representatives, tribunals and welfare agencies; safeguards against arbitrary eviction by a landlord are one example among many. Yet many people feel that freedom has diminished. What engenders this feeling is surely the remoteness in modern societies of those who exercise power. The eighteenth-century tenant could be evicted from his cottage at the squire's whim, but the squire was at least a human being with a place in the known scheme of things. He did not envisage his house being knocked down by a company that had bought it to build a railway, as in the nineteenth century, or by a council that had compulsorily purchased it to build a motorway, as in the twentieth. The deprivation of privacy here is the deprivation of identity—the sense of not being recognised as an individual, however humble, but merely as an obstacle to a scheme whose purposes far transcend the community.

Anxiety over privacy, therefore, begins with the transformation of society into large-scale, generally urban units, a process that went hand in hand with the Industrial Revolution. Privacy is associated in most people's minds with security—with being 'let alone' to live the kind of life and do the kind of work on which one had counted. This could be reconciled with the old custom of exposure by consent to one's neighbours, but not with the new exposure to powerful strangers. Life for the ordinary man was being turned upside down, and he felt himself to be naked and defenceless. It was the makers and possessors of the new wealth—factory-owners, mine-owners, rail-way entrepreneurs, urban landlords—who exercised a wholly unprecedented power over the lives of others. Dominant first and foremost in Britain, the cradle of the Industrial Revolution, this social process overtook other European countries and the United States in the course of the nineteenth century.

The paradox of the age (or one of its many paradoxes) was that its ruling ideology was that of individualism—the right to shape one's own life without social control, and to rebuff all inquisition with a sturdy 'Mind your own business and I'll mind mine'. This, it might be supposed, was the quintessence of privacy. The trouble was that the conditions of the industrial society, especially the intensive competition and the constant insecurity, threatened individualism at every point. It goes without saying that the benefits of individualism were largely denied to the poor, to those who owned nothing but their ability to work and had to place it at the disposal of their em-ployers. But the latter and the middle classes had their worries too—commercial failure or bankruptcy; disgrace through the operation of an increasingly rigid code of personal morals; exposure, whether of private or financial shortcomings, to a public that was no longer that of 'the neighbours' or 'county society' but, with the appearance of a national press, opinion at large.

Hence, the belief in individualism and the fragility of in-dividualism worked towards the same end—a desperate cling-ing to privacy and a truly neurotic fear of intrusion or dis-closure. It is remarkable how the theme of the 'deadly secret', to be guarded at all costs, runs through the literature of the nineteenth century, especially through best-selling novels (it had been relatively rare in the preceding century). The secret is the mainspring of *Jane Eyre*, *Adam Bede*, *Great Expectations*, *The Woman in White* and *The Master of Ballantrae*; with Dickens —the supreme popular author of the period, and a man with a well-kept secret of his own—it crops up in practically all his novels. Outside England the theme was less persistent, but it flowered handsomely in *Madame Bovary* and *Les Misérables*. Sometimes the secret belonged to the villain and earned the adjective 'guilty'. But, more often than not, it was the secret of a character, such as Rochester or Jean Valjean, with whom the reader was expected to sympathise (or, of course, of a wronged maiden).

So far, we have traced the threat to privacy in social forces in the broadest sense, and in private interests with the power to crush individuals. But as time goes on a new menace looms larger and larger—that of the State. With the growing complexity of society, and the increasing centralisation of economic activity, governments saw themselves obliged to assume greater responsibilities and greater powers. Individualism fought a bitter but inevitably a losing battle; there was ideological resistance to the census, to the income tax, to the establishment of the police force and of a professional civil service, to compulsory public health measures, to compulsory education, to laws about hours and conditions of work. By present-day standards, the intervention of the State in the affairs of the citizen was timid at any time before 1914. But it was seen as a ruthless and inexorable process, for it was in fact greater in each generation than in the one before.

Besides, the free-born Englishman had only to look across the Channel to observe shocking inroads by the State on privacy and on the liberties of the subject. Czarist Russia had internal passports, and most Continental countries had compulsory identity documents which had to be shown to the police on demand. All the major nations had conscription, involving control of the movements and residences of young men. Various governments, both of powerful empires and of petty Italian principalities, employed a political police with arbitrary powers to enter and search private homes.

By the 1930s, the State was seen as plainly the major threat to privacy and indeed as a devouring monster. The word 'totalitarian' was devised to refer to the Soviet Union, to Nazi Germany and to Fascist Italy. The common feature of these

regimes, and the justification for the label, was that the State
enforced its will in spheres which had hitherto been regarded
as private—in family life and the roles of men and women, in
the upbringing (as well as simply the education) of children,
in the use of leisure, in literature and the arts. There seemed
to be no corner at all where the individual could hide and be
let alone. Moreover, the State's demand for political con-
formity was so insistent that the citizen was not merely forbidden to express the 'wrong' opinions—this had been known
under tyrannical regimes throughout history—but obliged to
announce his adherence to the 'right' ones at every turn. And
with this went a horrifying extension of police power which
evoked in the English mind such gratifying reflections as 'At
least when I hear a knock at the door in the morning I know
it's the milkman'.

To many people, it began to look as though the twentieth-
century world was assuming a shape in which the advance of
the totalitarian State would be irresistible and its control of
every aspect of life would become the accepted norm. Nor did
these fears greatly recede after World War II. Hitler was de-
feated and dead, but freedom was still a puny plant in Germany
and Italy. Stalin was alive (until 1953) and the essentials of his
system were maintained by his successors. The United States
was swept in the early 1950s by the wave of intolerance associated with Senator Joseph McCarthy—inquisitions into private
lives which drove the victims to collapse or even suicide, black-
lists and dismissals, the demand for 'loyalty oaths' in State
employment and the universities. Even in Britain, economic
difficulties and the retention of wartime controls meant that
the State wielded powers never yet known in time of peace.
In some quarters, the post-war Labour Government's policies—
widespread nationalisation and new State-run welfare services
—together with such restrictions as building licences and planning permission, were seen as the harbingers of a new state of
affairs in which there would be no place for the private man.

The new technology, too, placed huge and novel powers at

the disposal of unscrupulous rulers. Radio had served Hitler as a potent medium of centralised propaganda, and was now reinforced by television. The work of the political police was eased by fingerprinting, by lie-detectors, by concealed listening devices and tape-recorders, to say nothing of new 'scientific' methods of torture. The computer was making its appearance, and it was getting easier and easier for the authorities to amass information about individuals; the US Federal Bureau of Investigation, by now more concerned with political minorities than with crime, was said to have files on 20 million Americans.

Once again, literature both reflected and influenced life. Science fiction, which had been innocently rhapsodic in the days of Jules Verne, was now in general pessimistic or frankly scarifying. And there was a notable change in the tone of the utopian novel. Formerly, this had been used (by William Morris in *News from Nowhere*, by H. G. Wells in a series of books) to paint a glowing picture of the happiness in store for mankind. But Aldous Huxley's *Brave New World*, published in 1932, gave a dire warning of total control of human life from the cradle (or rather the test-tube) to the grave and ruthless crushing of the deviant individual. Then, in 1949, came George Orwell's terrifying *1984*. Both the sales and the sensation were enormous, expressions such as 'Big Brother' passed into the language, and it is safe to say that very few works of the imagination have had so powerful and lasting effect on our thinking. Though the society depicted in *1984* was horrible in all its aspects, it was probably the total deprivation of privacy— made vivid by Orwell's invention of the 'telescreen' and by the phrase 'Big Brother is watching you'—that made the sharpest impact.

Are we, in reality, moving irresistibly toward '1984'? Now that we are within a decade of the actual date of 1984, and still living in a world more akin to that of 1949 than to Orwell's appalling vision, it may seem that we have been needlessly alarmed. Orwell, however, was not making a prediction but pointing to the logical outcome of trends that he observed

when he was writing. These trends are still at work. It is a fact
that the relentless progress of technology continues to create
greater powers of intrusion and surveillance. It is a fact that
the State is increasingly involved—often for benevolent purposes, but that is not necessarily a safeguard—in what used to
be thought of as private life. If nothing disastrous has happened
yet, we owe this to countervailing tendencies which are still
strong in British life (though weak or already vanquished in
many other countries). What we must always bear in mind is
that the price of privacy, like the price of liberty, is eternal
vigilance.

The setting up of the Younger Committee was an admission
on the part of authority that concern over privacy was real and
to some extent justified. However, two aspects of the story are
less reassuring. In the first place, the governments responsible
—both the Labour Government which appointed the Committee, and the Conservative Government which took office
before it seriously started work—were careful to exclude all
public bodies from its terms of reference. In other words, the
Committee was debarred from examining threats to privacy
coming from the State, from local government, from the police
or from any other source that could not be described as 'private
persons or organisations'. When the Committee sought clarification of this ruling, the only concession made was that it could
consider the BBC (public) on the same footing as independent
television and the press (private). The Younger Report, therefore, neglects a considerable—most people would say the
principal—sphere of its subject. Fortunately, this book is not
bound by that limitation.

Secondly, once the Committee had reported—and although
it made some specific proposals for new legislation—it was
observed that the Government was in no great hurry to do
anything about it. The Report, published in July 1972, was
not discussed in the House of Commons until July 1973; and
one MP remarked (and was not contradicted) that the reason
for holding a debate at that time was the recent affair involving

Lord Lambton, which had caused anxieties over press intrusion. When the Home Secretary, Mr Robert Carr, spoke in the debate, he was distinctly vague about the suggested legislation and altogether chilly about a law to 'establish a right of privacy' as a principle.

This question of a 'general right', as it has come to be called by those engaged in the argument, is of considerable importance; the case for it and the case against it will be set out later in this book. As soon as we begin to think about it, we become aware of the complexity that attends the whole subject. For, while most of us regard privacy as a value to be cherished in a society claiming to care about individual freedom, we also know that there are other values.

We accept nowadays that society—which in effect means the State and local government—should take responsibility for all sorts of things which in the past were left to economic forces or to private effort: for education, for the nation's health, for adequate housing, for employment opportunities, and so forth. This cannot be done without information about social needs and social demands. Moreover, plans have to be made well in advance; a mistake, even an error of omission, may be fatal in the sense that it cannot later be corrected. Take, for instance, a New Town. The people likely to settle there will include a high proportion of young men and women, unmarried or newly married. How many schools will be needed? It depends on how many children they are likely to have, which is a question of their wishes and intentions: what do they regard as a desirable family size? But it is also a question of what they do to ensure that these intentions become reality: will they employ contraception? How many of them are Catholics, and how many of the Catholics actually obey the rulings of their Church? It is obvious that any such inquiry touches on a sphere of life that people regard as the most private of all. A balance must be struck between the value of privacy and the value of having enough schools in ten years' time. This can, no doubt, be done in various ways; one can question a small sample, consisting of volunteers, instead of questioning everybody. But the problem exists, and must exist at every point in a society that is neither simple nor static.

So far, this is a matter of information concerning social groups; but in many contexts information is also required about individuals. Councils allocate housing on a basis of need, normally using an elaborate system of points (inadequacy of existing accommodation, family size, chronic illness or old age, and so on). Applicants have to disclose a good deal of personal information, and this information has to be verified. If a man has a cardiac weakness which makes it dangerous for him to climb stairs, the housing authority needs to know about it and will ask for a statement from his doctor; in strict theory, this at once violates the privacy of the relationship between doctor and patient. The same considerations apply to the various welfare benefits to which millions of people are entitled, and which a great many of them do not claim—sometimes through ignorance, sometimes because they dislike being questioned and investigated. Ought social workers to let these people live in unnecessary poverty, or press them to apply for the benefits in the knowledge that this will involve a surrender—perhaps embarrassing or painful—of privacy? Again, there are no simple answers.

Problems of a different nature, but no less tricky, are raised when the value of privacy has to be balanced against the value of publicity. One of the laudatory phrases applied to countries like Britain is 'the open society'; one of the citizen's most cherished rights is the right to know. As the Younger Report put it: 'A man's right to privacy has to be balanced against the rights of others; any additional protection which the law may afford to privacy may be found to impinge upon such other rights, in particular the right of free communication of the truth and of comment upon it, which are generally accepted as of great importance in a democratic society.'

As citizens, we rely on publicity to ensure that affairs are conducted in what we call an 'above-board' fashion, and to

mobilise opinion when they are not. The means of publicity
are, on a local scale, unfettered free speech in the pub or on the
village green, and at a public meeting; on a larger or a national
scale, the press, radio and television. This is how instances of
petty tyranny, injustice and corruption are brought into the
open. In the process, some pain is generally caused to the petty
tyrant, the unjust and the corrupt, but we normally regard
that as right and necessary. In a controlled, as opposed to an
'open', society—of which a characteristic feature is a monopoly
or censored press—all kinds of people are immune from unwelcome reporting and hostile comment. These include officials
and bureaucrats, police chiefs, and functionaries of the ruling
party; also, sometimes, wealthy private interests, able to buy
up or intimidate newspapers and to silence or get rid of 'irres-
ponsible agitators'. Most of us are clear in our minds that we
do not want to live in that kind of society.

Upholders of freedom, therefore, can find themselves cham-
pioning the right to know in one context and the right of
privacy in another. In a recent British case, when a journalist
was charged under the Official Secrets Act because he had
published a government report, it came out that bureaucrats
could ensure the secrecy of any document that might embarrass
them simply by stamping it 'Confidential'. The judge declared
that this was an unsatisfactory state of affairs, the journalist
was acquitted, and demands for a modification of this restric-
tive Act led the Government (inevitably) to set up a committee.
When its report (the Franks Report) was debated in Parliament, members from all parties stressed the need for a broader
right of publicity. Two weeks later, in the debate on the Younger
Report, members from all parties were pressing for new laws to
protect privacy. If we look to the United States, we find
Senator Sam Ervin of North Carolina conducting hearings on
privacy as Chairman of the Senate Sub-committee on Constitu-
tional Rights, and appearing a couple of years later to preside
over the considerably more famous Committee on the Water-
gate affair, whose role was to batter down official secrecy and

follow up allegations first made by inquiring newspapers. I am making no charge of inconsistency; I am drawing attention to two sets of values, both prized in a democratic society but not always easy to reconcile.

The borderline cases arise, particularly, with regard to aspects of private life that may or may not have public significance. The borough treasurer has taken a holiday that he cannot have been able to afford on his salary. He may have received a legacy or backed an outsider; is it our right to know? Councillor X of the planning committee and Mr Y, director of a building firm, had dinner together shortly before Mr Y's application came before the council; if a newspaper points this out, is it a relevant fact or an unfair innuendo and an intrusion on private social life? These are imaginary cases, but it will be well remembered that disclosures about personal friendships and personal gifts started the inquiries into the notorious Poulson affair. Generally, when guilt is proved, we applaud the press for its fearless investigations; when innocence is vindicated, we sympathise with the victim of snooping. But the press cannot know how things will turn out and has to proceed, in the first instance, on suspicion.

Then there is the question of the indisputably private life of a person who is 'in the public eye'. We take for granted that certain people—royalty, popular entertainers, politicians— have by definition forfeited the degree of privacy that the ordinary man expects. A pop star, for instance, must expect the world to know if he is charged with careless driving or possessing cannabis, if he is divorced or even temporarily separated from his wife. In return, he enjoys fame—indeed, he probably employs a publicity agent—and a high income. There are times, all the same, when he finds that the public is driving a hard bargain.

The trouble is that there are no firm rules about who is a public person, and for what purposes. Apparently, publicity is in order if a minister goes with a prostitute, but not if a back-bench MP does so. You can become a public person when, in your own eyes, you have not changed; for instance, when a surgeon carries out a transplant. You can be a public person through relationship, by having a famous father whom perhaps you never see, or by being seventeenth in succession to the throne. Worst of all, you can be catapulted into publicity in accidental and often highly distressing circumstances, for instance, if your baby is kidnapped.

For better or for worse—and in many respects it is certainly for the better—a society like ours is one in which there is a very wide range of public knowledge, public concern, and (at the simplest level) public interest. We have grown accustomed to living in such a society, and could not easily adapt ourselves to any other. Perhaps each of us wants privacy for himself and lack of privacy for other people. It is healthy for us, at all events, to recognise the ambiguity in our own attitudes and the difficulty of reducing the question of privacy to a simple yes-or-no issue.

Above all, privacy is a human matter. Respect for privacy, and violation of privacy, are aspects of how living, fallible people behave toward other people. These are statements of the obvious, but we miss a dimension of the problem unless we bear in mind that it concerns experiences of emotional significance— sometimes acute, sometimes profound.

It often seems—and not solely in the context of privacy— that we live nowadays in a world in which machines dominate people. This book will begin, necessarily, with a description of the new technology that has made the private man immensely more vulnerable. Ultimately, however, machines are the agents of human beings. The threat to privacy is a matter for each and all of us; so, I hope, is its defence.

PART ONE

The New Technology

TECHNIQUES OF INTRUSION

In its simplest sense, privacy is freedom from being seen or heard when one does not want to be. The law of trespass and the ancient statute which punishes 'Peeping Toms' are examples of legal protection for this kind of freedom. Such laws were made, however, when the only threats to privacy were the human eye and the human ear. They are supplemented nowadays by an immense variety of devices whereby the unsuspecting individual can be observed or photographed in an apparently lonely place or within four walls, can be heard when he thinks he is conducting a private conversation, and can also be heard when speaking on a private telephone line.

These devices, like weapons, are dangerous in proportion to the ways in which they are used. In reading about them, it should be borne in mind that the users may be:

(a) Agents of authority, police forces, government departments of various kinds. The menace is obviously greater under a dictatorial regime, which can follow up intrusion by arbitrary punishment without the risk of controversy or criticism, than in a democratic society. But events in several countries normally regarded as democratic should remind us that any authority is capable of injustice and of infringing individual rights.

(b) Employers, authorities in an autonomous institution such as a school or a hospital, and anyone whose position gives him power over the lives of others; also private security agencies and private detectives in the service of an employer or an institution.

26

(c) *Individuals seeking to injure other individuals, to pursue a vendetta, or simply to gratify idle curiosity and a perverted sense of fun, which may well cause considerable distress.*

It is in this context that we should consider techniques such as the following:

1 Alan F. Westin
TECHNOLOGICAL DEVICES

Fluorescent powders or dyes have been produced which are applied secretly to a person's hands, shoes, clothing, hair, umbrella, and the like, or can be added to such items as soap, after-shave lotion, and hair tonic which an individual applies to himself. Although these substances are invisible under regular light, they register as 'glowing' substances on the person being followed when he is illuminated by an ultraviolet-light source carried by the investigator.

A second locating device is the miniature radio-signal transmitter, smaller than a quarter. This is used at close ranges without antennae or is equipped with twelve to fifteen inches of thin wire antennae for longer-range shadowing. It can be secreted on a person, his clothing, car, or briefcase, or other articles that he carries. The transmitter sends out a signal which registers on a receiver tuned to that frequency, enabling the investigator to keep his quarry located, especially if two operatives are assigned to surveillance and a 'cross-fix' can be utilised. The places available for hiding such transmitters in a car are so plentiful that secret installation rarely presents a problem. In addition, surveillance manufacturers have built special auto-tagging equipment in the form of standard spotlights or rear-view mirrors.

Tagging transmitters can also be built into eyeglasses, hearing aids, and wrist watches for close-range shadowing. Longer-range transmitters (requiring some sort of antennae) have been made to match coat buttons, the antennae being sewed into the collar or piping of the garment. Shoes with shoelace antennae, tie-clasps with tie antennae, hat emblems with hatband antennae, and buckles with belt antennae are examples of how 'tagging' the individual has been carried out by resourceful investigators. The range of the signals with antennae is several city blocks.

Technology has recently contributed another advance on this front through the 'radio pill' developed for medical research. This emits a signal sufficiently strong to be followed at fairly close ranges—five to twenty yards today, with greater ranges expected in the near future. Thus, if a person takes large-sized anti-histamine or anti-allergy pills and an investigator can fill his medicine bottle with radio pills, a tag can be lodged in the stomach of the subject himself. It will eventually be passed out of the body without the individual's suspecting that he has been converted, for a time, into a living electronic beacon . . .

Today special 'screens' can be installed in the walls of a room that seem opaque to persons inside but permit an observer in the adjoining room to look through and photograph everything taking place. At the simplest level this is done by the well-known technique of using glass which seems to be a mirror or screen in the room under observation.

A far more sophisticated technique made possible by new technology is the use of special substances that seem to be wall panels and appear solid from both sides. These do not permit regular light to pass through, but transmit infra-red light— light with extra-long wave lengths—enabling investigators to take infra-red photographs or observe actions visually through an infra-red viewer. The infra-red light source does not have to be placed within the room; it can be supplied by a beam sent from the observation post itself.

Secreting cameras within a room has been a growing technique of the past two decades. Miniature 'still' cameras can be hidden within a room to take films on electronic signals from outside, at periodic pre-set intervals, or when triggered by a light switch being turned on or a file drawer opened. They can also be set off by the entrance of persons into an empty room, by means of antennae that sense changes in a room's

electronic balance. Electric eyes in these hidden cameras provide shutter changes to take account of light factors. Such
cameras, ranging in price from $100 to $300, are easily hidden
behind air-conditioning and heating grills, in wall clocks, in
the speaker section of television sets, and many other vantage
points. One radio-controlled model now in use by police and
private detectives can take more than four hundred 35-milli-
meter frames without reloading, from control distances of up to
one mile.

Probably the most useful device in visual surveillance is
closed-circuit television, since this provides continuous observation and permits instant response by the investigator to what is
seen. 'Television eyes' now come in small units (3 inches by
9 inches) commercially available at about $500. These can be
hidden on the premises and can send a picture of the room to
a remote receiver located a block or two away. TV cameras
have also been developed with light pipes, of optical fibers,
which can bend light around corners. Thus the camera can be
installed in another room and only the optic fibers need be
placed in the room under surveillance. TV cameras able to
fit into a vest pocker and featuring an 'eye' the width of a
cigarette have been built ever since the late 1950s and probably
for government surveillance work as well . . .

When persons are in a dark room, they may assume themselves to be immune from surveillance. The truth is that concealed cameras equipped with infra-red film can photograph
actions in a dark room if an invisible infra-red-energy source
has been placed within that room. One way this is done is by
putting special bulbs in overhead fixtures or lamps. To the
naked eye the bulb seems to be unlit, since no visible light is
transmitted; but it is actually flooding the room with infra-red
light and will provide the basis for clear snapshots or film. Of
course if the windows are bare, cameras outside the premises
can photograph inside by projecting infra-red illumination into
the room. Other cameras have methods of amplifying very
small visible-light sources. One closed-circuit television camera

operates with such sensitivity (and without the need of infra-red energy) that it can transmit clear pictures of an entire room from the illumination of a cigarette lighter.

__While some persons seek privacy in closed or darkened rooms, others go out along public streets or parks or place themselves considerable distances away from other persons or objects. Several types of camera devices enable investigators to handle these situations. Miniature still cameras costing less than $100 have been made in the form of cigarette lighters or match boxes; with these, or a regular miniature camera concealed in the palm of the hand or in a hat, a casual passerby or a man sitting across the aisle on a bus can take pictures of his 'subject' without detection.

Telephoto-lens cameras will produce a clear picture of a person 100 yards away. Special lenses with extra-long focal length (costing $1,000 or less) can produce recognisable pictures of persons from 500 to 1,000 yards away . . .

The investigator's dream is to make his subject a walking radio transmitter, enabling the investigator to hear everything the subject says to anyone else, or even what he mutters aloud while he walks along the street. This can be done by wiring a person's clothing. A leading method is to build a microphone into one button of a suit coat, a sub-miniature transmitter into a second button, and the batteries into a third. The thread with which the special buttons are sewn in is of conductive wire, carried through the seams of the coat or jacket to make up the antenna. Access to the subject's coat for a few minutes is all that is necessary to install these devices. Common points of contact—the tailor shop, the dry-cleaning establishment, the restaurant checkroom, and the like—are often available. An example of the installation possibilities of existing micro-miniature transmitters is provided by a transmitter so small that it has been mounted as a tooth in a dental bridge.

Because of the expense and frequent difficulty of wiring the person, plus the fact that the place of conversations to be overheard is often known in advance, wiring the premises is the most common form of eavesdropping. Developments in electronics and miniaturisation in the past two decades, moving from the vacuum tubes of the 1930s to transistors and the latest 'chip' integrated circuits, have reduced bugging devices to ultra-miniature sizes. Microphones the size of sugar cubes ($10) or special 'pea' units ($100) are presently available to secrete in rooms, offices, autos, chairs in hotel lobbies, tables at bars and restaurants, and so forth. By 1966 micro-miniaturisation had reduced high-quality microphones to match-head size.

Any of the tiny mikes presently available can be attached by adhesive to the underside of furniture or by magnetic force to metal objects. They can also be installed inside telephones, intercoms, doorbell units, radios, TVs, water coolers, desk sets, clocks, picture frames, lamps, mattresses, flower pots, ash trays, cellophane-tape dispensers, bulletin boards, air conditioners, and a hundred other common objects within the room. A special microphone and transmitter have been built into a light bulb so that the transmitter begins broadcasting when the light switch is turned on and stops when it is turned off.

Usually microphones are attached to the regular electrical wiring system or have their own wires connected to a receiver outside the room. Common models of this type have a range of one to three city blocks and cost $135 to $250. At the listening post the eavesdropper can monitor the conversation and make a tape recording of the parts he desires. Battery-operated portable tape recorders provide one to six hours of recording time without change of tape. Special equipment is available which activates a tape recorder automatically when voices are heard in the room and shuts it off when conversation ceases; this makes it unnecessary to 'man' a listening post. Tape recorders with twenty-four hours or more of recording time are used by surveillance specialists. Miniature tape recorders providing a full hour without changing the reel have been reduced to cigarette pack size.

Where utmost security is called for, investigators use trails of electrically conductive metallic paint from the microphone, along the walls or baseboards, and out to the receiver location or a place safe enough to connect to regular wires. The paint trails can be sprayed with artificial dust so that they don't look fresher than the old paint surfaces ...

If a room is not closed completely—as when a window is open—directional microphones are able to zoom in and pick up speech at a considerable distance—across a city street, for example. Simple and easily operated parabolic microphones with eighteen-inch discs are advertised in the general press today as 'toys' and have tested out as effective for ranges of 500 to 600 feet. These cost $15 to $20. Larger directional microphones increase this range considerably.

In addition to beaming through windows into rooms, directional microphones are used to listen to conversations outdoors —for example, on park benches or in fields hundreds of feet from any other object. Conversations in rowboats on a lake, as parties walk along a street, or as people dine at an outdoor restaurant terrace have been recorded through use of directional microphones. A special gun developed for American military authorities can shoot a small dart containing a wireless radio microphone into a tree, window pane, clump of bushes, awning, or any other object near people whose conversation the investigator wants to overhear.

SOURCE: Alan F. Westin. *Privacy and Freedom* (1970)

2 R. V. Jones
THE 'HARMONICA BUG'

A still more remarkable device is what is known as the 'Harmonica Bug'. Once this is installed in the telephone of the victim, the eavesdropper, who can be anywhere, even thousands of miles away, provided that he is on a direct dialing system, merely dials the victim's number and blows a predetermined musical note on a harmonica. This note is picked up by the device in the victim's telephone, and prevents it from ringing.

At the same time it connects the telephone microphone into the line so that the eavesdropper can listen to any conversations that are taking place within earshot of the victim's telephone. Prices of such instruments range from $400 to $1,000.

SOURCE: R. V. Jones. *Some Threats of Technology to Privacy*, a paper quoted in the *Report* of the Secretary-General of the United Nations on Human Rights and Scientific and Technological Development to the Commission on Human Rights (E/CN4/1028, 1970)

3 Louis B. Sohn
MINI TRANSMITTERS

A dentist, while filling a tooth cavity, might have inserted there a miniature microphone capable of transmitting every word spoken by the person concerned during the day; or the dentist might have inserted in the tooth a small transmitter emitting a signal permitting an operator in a distant room to follow closely the person's movements all over a city. Similarly, a transmitter hidden in a car permits another person to follow that car easily regardless of all evasive manoeuvres.

SOURCE: Louis B. Sohn. *Science, Technology and Human Rights*, quoted in UN *Report*, 1970

4 Stanley M. Beck
MINI RECORDERS

A contact microphone (lima-bean size) can be attached to the opposite side of a wall in the room. When sound waves set up by speech strike the wall, the contact mike picks up enough of the vibration to permit accurate recording. When the walls are too thick, a variation on the contact microphone, a 'spike-mike' is used. The vibrations are transmitted through spikes 'the size of a small nail' to contact mikes and then recorded.

The most sophisticated development for recording speech

from a closed room is a tiny device that uses a reflector made of a thin diaphram and a microwave antenna. The device is activated by a microwave beam that goes through solid walls and has a range of a city block. When activated it sends the vibrations in the room to an outside receiver and the conversation is recorded.

SOURCE: Stanley M. Beck. 'Electronic Surveillance and the Administration of Criminal Justice', in *Canadian Bar Review*, quoted in UN *Report*, 1970

5 Younger Report
COMPREHENSIVE LIST OF SURVEILLANCE DEVICES

Devices for visual surveillance

Device	Capability and other characteristics
Observing only	
(a) magnifying (or telescopic) lens (with or without camera):	no practical limit to magnification; normal size print can be read at hundreds of yards.
(b) light intensifier (with or without camera):	normal vision in poor daylight or moonlight; acceptable vision on an overcast, moonless night.
(c) image stabilisation (this does for the image received by the lens what the human eye does automatically, so it would normally be used with a camera):	allows sharp pictures to be obtained from helicopters or by hand, even walking around.
(d) scanner to read contents of envelopes:	a needle-thin flash-light can be inserted in a sealed envelope to illuminate the contents for quick reading by a trained investigator; or the carbon in the print or ink of the message can be reflected by infra-red energy.
Recording	
(e) cameras, 'still' or motion, with an ordinary lens and using film of different sensitivities and grains; or also using the devices	lens magnification is the main means of taking pictures at a distance, but the quality of the picture depends a lot also on the sensitivity and grain (fineness) of the film used; the latter

Device	Capability and other characteristics
at (a), (b), (c) and (f): a camera using the devices at (a), (b) and (c) can be a television camera, that is, a camera which transmits the image by radio waves as it films (a picture taken on infra-red film (f) could, after processing, be transmitted in the same way); cameras can be operated by remote control:	particularly governs the definition of any enlarged pictures made from the film.
(f) infra-red film (the infra-red illumination of the object is sensed by the emulsion of the film, so this works only with a camera):	still or moving pictures of excellent definition can be taken in the dark.

Devices for aural surveillance

Device	Capability and other characteristics
Listening only	
(g) microphone using wired link, the wired link either being specially laid or using existing pair of wires or single insulated wire; can also be applied like a stethoscope to listen to sounds on the other side of a wall:	range and sensitivity in effect unlimited depending on size of the microphone; certainly able to be superior to the human ear; a microphone about the size of a match head can pick up a whisper at 20 feet.
(h) microphone using radio link, i.e. a microphone coupled to a radio transmitter; this is the proverbial 'bug', intruded in many ways, e.g. in a cocktail olive, a cuff link, tiepin, telephone, dart shot into a wall:	sensitivity of the microphones as (g) above; size, including battery, of a lump of sugar; practical transmission range about a quarter of a mile.
(i) tap on a telephone line—this can be a metallic contact, but this is not necessary, as an induction device which picks up the pulses in the line is equally effective; these draw an almost undetectable amount of electricity from the telephone wire and give no betraying noises:	reception just as good as the telephone user's; can be applied at any point on the line, indoors or out.

Device	Capability and other characteristics
(j) 'infinity transmitter', a device inserted into a telephone handset, which, when activated by dialling the number and giving an ultrasonic note on the last digit, prevents the telephone ringing and transmits over the dialler's telephone line all the sounds in the room where the telephone is situated, whether the handset is on or off the telephone:	can be installed in three minutes; reception just as good as the telephone used properly; but works only on telephones with direct Post Office lines; that is, not through a switchboard.
(k) induction device to pick up telephone conversations from the stray magnetic field of the telephone itself:	must be within about 4 feet of the telephone.
(l) directional (or 'parabolic' or 'telescopic') microphone concentrating a beam of sound from a distance onto a sensitive microphone and so hearing across intervening noises:	range about 25 yards; rather bulky and so difficult to conceal, and background noise can interfere.
(m) invisible light beams for monitoring vibrations, usually spoken of in the context of the laser; the vibrations can be sensed on any object near the speaker, including a window pane if it is coated with an invisible metallic film:	there is lack of agreement about the capability of these; it does not appear that they yet exist in any marketable form.
Recording	
(n) tape recorder: in addition to ancillary use as noted below, miniature tape recorders can themselves be concealed on premises or person, and so record sounds directly:	sensitivity as for (g) and (h); can be no larger than a packet of cigarettes, depending on size can record anything fed to it; one tape can accommodate 16 hours' recording.
(o) sound filtration, to pick out one sound from another simultaneous one, for example a conversation from a mixture of sounds including traffic noise or a radio played deliberately to obscure the conversation:	some extraneous noise can be filtered out mechanically or electronically depending on the circumstances.

Devices for tailing

Device	Capability and other characteristics
(p) trail 'bug' emitting a signal which enables a person to be tailed if it can be secreted on or in his person or vehicle:	as 'bugs' of this kind are swallowed for medical purposes it follows the smallest are no bigger than a medicine capsule; range from a few feet to a few miles depending on size.
(q) low-level radioactive powders administered to the person being tailed; trailer follows with a geiger counter:	range of 200–300 yards.
(r) fluorescent dyes, applied to a person being tailed, which are reflected when subjected to an ultraviolet light source:	these can be applied in soaps, lotions or to clothing; range depends on range of ultra-violet light source which would tend to be short.

SOURCE: *Report of the Committee on Privacy* (1972)

American writers have given many examples of the use of such devices by police forces, the Federal Bureau of Investigation, the Internal Revenue Service, the Defense Department, and other official bodies. And in Britain:

6 Donald Madgwick
POLICE USE OF BUGGING DEVICES

There is growing evidence that the police force uses bugging devices for crime detection. In 1959 in Newcastle-under-Lyme a secretly recorded conversation was produced in court and as a result a man was found guilty of assaulting a woman and fined £5. In 1966 the Bradford police used a bug in a murder investigation. Two suspects were invited to the Town Hall for questioning and were left alone together. Their conversation was recorded by a device hidden in a waste paper basket. It included incriminating statements which were used in evidence and they were convicted of murder. In December 1967 the police in Hackney used a bug to secure evidence against a

Council employee accused of intimidation and corruption. In March 1966 the *Sun* reported an experiment in a south coast town where detectives had been equipped with miniature microphones concealed in a buttonhole or cuff link and recorders carried in a shoulder holster. It was quoted as having 'quite astonishing results' and a number of men were arrested on house breaking charges. C. H. Rolph in an article entitled 'The Threat to Privacy' described a 'crime prevention stunt' where two Portsmouth detectives, apparently wearing milk bottle tops in their caps as badges, disguised themselves as water board officials and gained entrance to ten houses in the area. They taped conversations and when alone in a room searched for hidden savings. The operation was filmed without the housewives' knowledge and shown on a Southern Television programme *Crime Desk*. The object was to show people how dangerous it was to hide money in the house and how easy it would be for a thief to steal it.

SOURCE: Donald Madgwick. *Privacy Under Attack* (National Council for Civil Liberties, 1968)

Finally, it is important to take note of the growing availability and cheapness of these devices, the confident sales methods used to push them, and the evident appeal that they make. In almost all countries, the selling and possession of the devices is perfectly legal; only their use may be held illegal in certain circumstances.

7 Alan F. Westin
BUGGING DEVICES ON SALE IN THE USA

The most blatant campaign aimed at the general public is the activity of the Continental Telephone Supply Company, with stores in such cities as New York, Philadelphia, and Miami, and national direct-sale newspaper advertising. Continental features telephone monitors ('Just think of the uses . . . !') and miniature recording devices ('to record unobserved and secretly'), equipped with 'tieclasp microphone.' When a Con-

tinental Telephone Supply store opened recently in Miami, its invitation read:

> Big Brother is going to have his own department store. You are cordially invited to attend the opening of a unique new store designed to cater to members of our suspicious society . . . This new retail outlet offers the very latest in telephone bugging devices, spy cameras, probes that can pick up voices through walls, lamps that are actually radio transmitters, disguised tape recorders and a host of other electronic privacy invaders.

SOURCE: Alan F. Westin. *Privacy and Freedom* (1970)

8 UN Report
USE OF BUGGING DEVICES
IN THE NETHERLANDS

Technical means of interfering with privacy are being continually improved. As a result of mass production and relatively low prices, such devices are becoming more and more widely used. All modern sales promotion techniques are being used to encourage their distribution, and to arouse interest in them in circles where no such interest previously existed.

This would not be particularly important in itself, if it did not reflect a latent demand for such devices. It is clear that many persons are now anxious to keep watch on the private lives of others. In addition, the use of these new technical devices has some of the elements of a game; and this also attracts many people.

SOURCE: Government of the Netherlands Report, quoted in UN *Report*, 1970

9 Donald Madgwick
BUGGING DEVICES FOR SALE IN BRITAIN

The *Birmingham Mail* recently carried the advertisement: 'For sale in Birmingham. Listen to conversations up to 50 yards away without the person's knowledge (like the spies use). Dangerous? Yes, but what fun. Only 19 guineas each.' It brought an immediate protest from the Midlands group of the NCCL, which pointed out the danger that this type of 'bug' might be used for blackmail and industrial espionage, besides being a gross infringement of individual privacy.

Even more recently, an American manufacturer, Mr Ben Jamil of New York, was refused a licence to demonstrate a range of 'bugging' devices at the US Trades Fair in London. The then Postmaster General, Mr Anthony Wedgwood Benn, ruled that it would be 'undesirable' to show them. But Mr Jamil was undeterred, and promptly announced his intention of bringing his wares to Britain for open sale over the counter. One of his devices—he had 75 in all—could allow an industrialist in Zurich to listen into a board meeting of his rivals in London. It could operate over any distance from any automatic telephone.

SOURCE: Donald Madgwick. *Privacy under Attack* (NCCL, 1968)

10 Younger Report
DEVICES AVAILABLE IN BRITAIN

One firm of private detectives provided us with copies of its sales catalogue. It gave details of radio microphones, telephone transmitters, recorders and receivers, and a device designed to operate in a telephone circuit so as automatically to switch on and off a tape recorder, and other equipment designed for when the telephone is in use. Some microphones were illustrated disguised as a box of matches, a cuff link, a fountain pen and a lapel badge. A security adviser to a large firm showed us a microphone designed as a wrist-watch. A firm of security consultants demonstrated a wide range of devices, including an infra-red viewer for night surveillance, telephone line tapping equipment and a magnetic microphone.

SOURCE: *Report of the Committee on Privacy* (1972)

UNDER ASSESSMENT

This section deals with a scientific—or pseudo-scientific, for its value is highly controversial—development peculiar to the last few decades. Employers, when considering applicants for jobs, have always tried to evaluate such intangibles as 'character' and 'reliability' as well as competence to do the actual work. The recent tendency is to have recourse to personality tests, originally designed for clinical work by psychologists, in an effort to decide who is suitable and who is not. In some cases the testing is imposed not only on new applicants but on existing employees, who may on this basis be transferred to other work, promoted or refused promotion, perhaps discovered to be unsuitable and dismissed. The indications supplied by the tests reach deeply into personal life, and the implications for privacy need no stressing.

11 Arthur R. Miller
PERSONALITY TESTS

Tests seeking to evaluate emotional stability and personality traits, although more sparingly used than aptitude, intelligence, and achievement tests, raise more serious privacy issues. Unlike the comparatively emotion-free responses called for by skill measuring tests, the product of a personality inventory typically is a series of verbal or sensory responses that are highly subjective in character and often reveal the innermost feelings of the person under examination. Let the questions speak for themselves; the following inquiries or variations on them are found on many widely used personality tests:

Have you ever engaged in sexual activities with another man or boy (asked of male subjects)?

When you were a youngster, did you engage in petty thievery?

Are you troubled by the idea that people on the street are watching you?

Do you think something is wrong with your sex organs?

D

Do you think that Jesus Christ was greater than Lincoln or
Washington?
Once in a while do you think of things too bad to talk about?
Are you a special agent of God?

Moreover, in contrast to the relative ease of scaling IQ or
aptitude-test responses, meaningful appraisal of personality test
results requires analysis by a highly trained person. Even then
the evaluation may be inaccurate or misleading because of the
inherent unreliability or unsuitability of the test, the un-
representative frame of mind or emotional state of the subject
when taking the test, the physical environment in which the
test was given, or the demeanor or attitude of the individual
who administered it. For example, in one case described to a
congressional committee, a female government employee was
questioned for six hours 'about every aspect of her sex life—
real, imagined, and gossiped—with an intensity that could
only have been the product of inordinately salacious minds.'
One wonders whether such an interrogation could possibly
yield an accurate index of the personality of the examinee.

Yet the actual utilisation of psychological testing takes no
cognisance of these important considerations or the dubious
character of many currently fashionable tests. Wide-ranging
and intrusive psychological inventories often are purchased in
bulk from publishing companies for pennies a copy and administered indiscriminately to job applicants. In many cases
this is done without expert advice concerning the test's suit-
ability for measuring particular personality traits or for evaluating an individual's responses. The cut-out stencil score sheets
furnished by many publishers simplify the effort and encourage
total thoughtlessness on the part of the tester. As strange as it
may sound, many personnel managers are purporting to pass on
the level of an individual's 'neuroticism,' 'alienation,' 'drive,'
and 'stability,' by a process that often is not appreciably more
scientific than measuring the size and shape of the subject's
head. As Martin L. Gross has indicated, we are passively watch-

ing business and government conduct a nationwide quest for the Square American; their divining rod is a selection of tests that more than not merely reflect the biases of their creators, thereby perversely giving a premium to those examination subjects who know how to psych the psycher.

The potential dangers to individual privacy from misuse of raw psychological test data are obvious. Disclosure of the individual's responses to sensitive questions or over-all scores might cause him acute embarrassment as well as professional and economic injury. Moreover, these items can easily be misconstrued since they have significance only to highly trained professionals. Even in the hands of competent personnel, individual responses are meaningful only when examined in the framework of the entire examination and in light of the purpose for which it was administered.

For similar reasons the analysis ultimately distilled from the raw data by a trained psychologist may be a threat to the individual if it is not handled with circumspection. The preservation and circulation of the evaluator's cryptic, but derogatory sounding, comments, such as 'unstable,' 'deviant,' or 'unmotivated,' can haunt the test subject throughout his life. There is the related danger that untrained management personnel may draw and publicise unwarranted inferences from a professional appraisal. This danger is heightened if the test report was prepared for extremely narrow purposes or only to be used by other professionals. Substantial additional prejudice could result from reliance on evaluations in contexts beyond those for which the test originally was administered or from their retention for such protracted periods that they no longer reflect the attitudes and emotional make-up of the subjects. These are not hypothetical risks, because most firms retain their employees' test records as part of their permanent files. In some ways, even retesting would be more sensible than relying on aged data.

Going beyond the threat to individual privacy, if psychological testing gains too prominent a position in the decision-

making process, it may begin to create substantial risks to
society at large. The primary virtue of personality tests supposedly lies in their ability to describe an individual's mental
capacity and emotional balance or to predict his future
behavior. Unless highly accurate extensive reliance, on these
tests may lead to the stratification of groups according to their
examination results as well as the erroneous allocation and
utilisation of human resources. It is possible, for example, that
a child who does poorly on aptitude tests in the first and second
grades will be given less attention by the teacher, or placed in a
slower section for instructional purposes, and, as a result, may
have a substantially lowered chance of performing well on a
college entrance examination ten years later.

SOURCE: Arthur R. Miller. *The Assault of Privacy* (1972)

12 Alan F. Westin
PERSONALITY TESTS

The basic objection on privacy grounds to the typical personality test used in personnel selection today—with its questions on such topics as sex and political values—is that many
individuals do not want to be sorted and judged according to
standards that rest on the unexplained evaluations of professional psychologists in the employ of 'institutional' clients.
Liberals fear that a government or industrial psychologist will
enforce conformist or elitist norms. Conservatives fear that
school or government testing might not only 'reward' liberal
ideology and penalise conservative ideas but also 'implant'
ideas through the testing process itself. Negroes are concerned
that psychologists might enforce standards of personality that
penalise minority groups and that the personality test might
enable the 'white power structure' to accomplish covertly discrimination it can no longer carry out openly. In all these
situations the assertion of privacy serves to say to those in
power: 'If you make evaluative decisions openly, questioning

me directly and justifying your decisions openly, I can fight out publicly your right to judge me in a certain way, and American society will decide our conflicting claims. But if you invoke "science" and "expertise" and evaluate me through personality tests, the issue becomes masked and the public cannot judge the validity and morality of these evaluative decisions. Thus, where such basic issues as political ideology, religion, and race are at stake, the selection process must be objective and public, and I assert my right of privacy to close my emotions, beliefs, and attitudes to the process of job evaluation in a free society.'

In addition, the basic aim of test psychology is admittedly to search for norms of conduct and to use these for judgment in 'trait' and 'prediction' matters. The intellectuals who lead the anti-personality-testing campaigns know how far they themselves are from any type of 'bland' normality, how many conflicts and personal disturbances lie behind their social masks, and yet how useful they are in their area of work, whether it is business, law, government, teaching, or the ministry. Many intellectuals are aware of the test psychologist's answer that he does not advise the selection of 'normals' only, that the tests can reward imagination, initiative, and other traits. But, knowing how fundamentally emotional tension and creativity are linked in the individual, intellectuals are not willing to submit themselves or the majority of their fellow citizens to the judgment of psychologists on that point. One of the basic functions of privacy is to protect the individual's need to choose those to whom he will bare the true secrets of his soul and his personality. The counseling and clinical psychologists have long been among the handful of those professional groups in whom many Americans have been willing to place such intimate trust. If civic reactions of the 1960s are any sign of developing public trends, many will not accept the test psychologist, working for an institutional client, in such a role.

Finally, from the literature of psychology and psychiatry, as well as from personal experience, critics of personality testing know that many individuals go through life with personal problems and conflicts that they keep under control. These 'managed' conflicts may involve sex, struggles over self-image, careers, and similar matters. Most of these people can grow old without having these conflicts become serious enough to impair their capacities at work, in the family, or as citizens. If these capacities are impaired, of course, the individual needs help; he may seek it himself, or it may be offered to him when his difficulties become observable. The problem presented by the spread of personality testing is that it may, by the pressures of testing and of rejection in selection, bring to the surface personality conflicts that might otherwise never have become critical in the individual's life, and may thus precipitate emotional crises.

SOURCE: Alan F. Westin. *Privacy and Freedom* (1970)

The Director-General of the International Labour Office has written:

13 Director-General, ILO
PREJUDICIAL RESULTS OF TESTS

There is evidence that testing may discriminate against culturally disadvantaged groups. Such discrimination may sometimes be intentional, though generally it is likely to be due to the simple fact that individuals who are culturally disadvantaged or belong to minority cultural groups are often handicapped when competing with others in certain types of tests. There is here a potential, if unintended, abuse of testing which can be eliminated only if testing procedures are devised which can accommodate a diversity of cultural backgrounds.

Secondly, tests and interview techniques which seek to penetrate personality and measure such imponderables as emotions, attitudes, mental equilibrium, adaptability, or capacity to withstand psychological stress may be designed to have the subject reveal his political views or his attitudes on intimate religious, political, sexual or family matters; a candidate, or even his family, may be subjected to gruelling interviews and other tests placing him under great mental stress and he may be under observation without even being aware of it. The conclusions derived from tests designed to penetrate an individual's subconscious and to make him reveal things about himself which bear no direct relation to his future employment may be of dubious validity, particularly if the tests are conducted and analysed by persons who are not highly qualified psychiatrists and psychologists. An individual's whole career may be compromised, and his morale unnecessarily shaken, by undependable or meaningless scores in such tests. The employer or person who decides not to employ the worker may come into possession of a mass of actual or inferred information of a highly personal nature about him which is not related to his work. Is not the whole question of the relationship to personal freedom of the encroachment of promotion and selection techniques upon privacy another issue of substantial importance for the discharge of our commitment to personal freedom?

These issues have been made much more acute by current developments in information storage. Prejudicial information, whether unfair or misleading or not unfair but irrelevant or best forgotten, has become much more serious because much less likely to be forgotten or overlooked.

SOURCE: *Report* of the Director-General, International Labour Office (Geneva, 1972)

Professor Westin quotes an individual experience:

14 Alan F. Westin
A TEST TAKER'S RIGHT TO PRIVACY

In January, 1965, an autobiographical article titled 'Adventures of a Test Taker' appeared in the *National Review*. It related the experiences of a woman who had refused, on privacy grounds, to answer the 'complete-a-sentence' questions asked her by an unnamed major federal agency about such things as her sex life, her religion, and her parents' private lives. Though the woman was found by the personnel department to be excellent material for the job and she had already begun working, the medical department of the agency considered her refusal to answer all the questions as a psychological danger sign and ordered her to take a two-day battery of additional tests, ranging from the Minnesota Multiphasic to the draw-a-figure test and the Rorschach ink-blot test. She then was interviewed by three doctors, who assured her that the testing was all for her own good, and asked further questions about whether, being a Catholic, she saw visions or heard voices and how she handled her sex drives. When she maintained that the tests were invalid instruments, gave 'phony results,' and invaded her privacy (she had taken psychology courses in college and had read Gross's book), the head of the medical department, a psychiatrist, told her that the department would not let her 'get away with this.' The woman was dismissed from the agency on orders of the medical department, and in the course of being checked out, she was told of numerous other instances in which persons found to be wholly satisfactory by the personnel officers had been forced to leave by the medical division. The author concluded that the personality testers were tightening their hold over this agency and were pursuing a policy of forced self-invasions of privacy that posed a serious threat to the citizen and the nation:

> The basic question, of course, is whether, under any circumstances, any employer has the right to the intimate details of his employees' personal lives. There is a certain point beyond which we may not go in violating the privacy of an individual, even if we say we are protecting our security or increasing our efficiency . . . We accept testing as voluntary. Yet even psychiatrists admit that the questions asked on psychological questionnaires are cleverly designed to trap the subject into revealing subconscious attitudes and reactions of which he himself may not be aware. Is this so different from the use of truth serum? Is it not the right to privacy and indeed, personality, which is really at stake?

SOURCE: Alan F. Westin. *Privacy and Freedom* (1970)

A particular variety of the personality test is the 'reactive assessment' :

15A UN Report
REACTIVE ASSESSMENT

The form of personality assessment permitting the greatest degree of voluntary control by the person concerned over what he reveals is called reactive, obtrusive assessment. Reactive assessment requires that the person being assessed make a choice as to whether or not he or she wishes to participate in that assessment. If that choice is negative, then reactive assessment cannot proceed. Either obtrusive or unobtrusive measurement may take place in the context of this assessment. Obtrusive measurement occurs whenever the respondent knows what aspect of his responses is crucial for the assessment. For instance, in a survey of political attitudes, the subject of the assessment may be whether or not one is in favour, say, of one's country adopting a certain policy. A reply of 'yes' or 'no' to a straightforward question on that topic in fact determines what is regarded as one's attitude.

There are many reactive assessment procedures, however, that have unobtrusive elements that may be of paramount interest for the assessor. A large variety of such indirect approaches within a reactive assessment have been developed. In an interview, for instance, which the person to be interviewed has consented to give, the assessment may really be not specifically concerned with what that person says but with how long the response takes, with eye gaze, eye blinks, vocal tone and amplitude and the like. Or, on a personality test, assessment experts might consider the length of time involved in taking the test—whether answers were crossed out, whether items were changed by the respondent to make them less ambiguous, whether items phrased in the first person were answered differently from those phrased in the third person, and so on.

Even factual questions, apparently measuring a person's knowledge of economic statistics, have been used to measure, for
example, allegiance as between management and labour
unions. It was assumed in this study that generally persons
would be ignorant of the actual statistics concerning average
earnings, profits and the like so that the direction of error in
over-estimating labour's wages or under-estimating corporate
profits would betray a person's fundamental sympathies. In
short, unobtrusive measurement, in a reactive context, typically
involves varying degrees of deception as to what the assessment
is either stated or be or might reasonably be presumed to be
about.

This account then goes on to describe the 'non-reactive assessment' :

15B UN Report
NON-REACTIVE ASSESSMENT

Unobtrusive, non-reactive assessment approaches occur when
the person does not know that he is revealing some aspect of his
wishes, interests, beliefs, values or, more generally, his personality. Furthermore, this exhibition occurs without the person
having given any consent, informed or otherwise, to parti-
cipating in a psychological assessment. Typically the evidence
accumulated in this manner is in a public setting that provides
useful information of an anonymous sort. For instance, studies
have been done in museums of the erosion of floor tiles to get a
cumulative record of what exhibits people most often visit.

Theatre audiences have been studied with sophisticated
electronic hardware to detect the extent of fidgeting—a pre-
sumptive index of boredom or under-interest. One study used
an electromagnetic movement meter involving an oscillator
detector, a DC amplifier, and an Esterline Angus ink-writing
recorder. A concealed copper screen located behind the subject's head was sensitive to the subject's movements and trans-
lated this information into electronically recorded impulses.

Respiratory reactions also have been used to study reactions to films but practical difficulties make this kind of assessment more effective in the controlled conditions of a laboratory. As an example of the prevalence—if not the technological sophistication—of unobtrusive, non-reactive research in public places, may be cited a study carried out in 1965, in which a scientist sitting with a press card in the gallery, recorded 3,322 interactions among representatives at meetings of the Administrative and Budgetary Committee of the United Nations General Assembly. Each interaction was coded for location, initiator, presence or exchange of documents, apparent humour and duration. The research interest was in identifying clusters of nations that typically interact.

A further example of psycho-physiological personality assessment is a technique that purports to reveal 'private attitudes about public things and persons'. This approach examines changes in the contraction or dilation of the pupil of the eye when the person concerned is presented with pictures. In one study, for instance, pictures of leading political figures were used. This study reports that one out of three of those professing preference for one of two major candidates in a political campaign actually preferred the other candidate, preference being indicated by pupil dilation for preferred candidates and pupil contraction for disapproved candidates. Work has been done on reactions to verbal materials as well.

SOURCE: *Report* of the UN Secretary-General on Human Rights and Scientific and Technological Development (E/CN4/1116, 1973)

There is nothing even faintly illegal about the use of these tests, and it is steadily increasing, notably in international companies with employees of various nationalities. However, there is hope. Professor Westin was told by one company that it has given up personality assessment after finding that the boss was totally unsatisfactory for employment.

THE COMPUTER REVOLUTION

The last two sections have dealt with ways in which information (accurate or not) is secured; we have now to look at the ways in which it is accumulated and used. The human memory has been reinforced for thousands of years by writing, and over the last 100 years by typing and mimeographing. The invention of the computer has facilitated the storage and handling of information to a degree that can fairly be called revolutionary. Its effects can be summarised in three ways:

Firstly, the amount of information that can be accumulated is no longer limited by the storage space needed for masses of sheets of paper and metal cabinets, nor by the labour and wages of clerks and typists. The Bible, for instance, can be reproduced on a thin sheet of plastic less than two inches square. It is therefore feasible to include far more items (or 'bits' in computer jargon) than in the past. Also, computerised records are more durable than pieces of paper, and there is no incentive to get rid of them after a limited period of time. With regard to records concerning individuals, the scope for the invasion of privacy is greatly enlarged.

Secondly, information is more likely to be centralised—both because this is easy, and because computers are too expensive for small local organisations. Formerly, a man's medical record was kept in his doctor's surgery and his employment record in the National Insurance office, both in his home town. Now, records can be collected in a computerised data-bank containing millions of items and operating on a nation-wide scale.

Thirdly, it is no longer necessary for those who seek information from the records to write a letter and wait for an answer. A phone call will produce a swift response from the data-bank, and it is also possible for computers to be linked so that one of them 'questions' another. This eliminates not only delay, but also the opportunity for a man-made decision as to whether the divulging of the information is justified. The pace at which computers work is the most rapidly advancing aspect of the computer revolution. From 25,000 calculations per second in 1955 it is, expected to reach 1,000 million per second in 1975.

To describe this state of affairs more fully, we turn in the first place to developments in the United States.

16A Alan F. Westin
PROBES AND DOSSIERS IN THE USA

The mobility of persons and the standardisation of life in mass society have led to the development of large private and governmental investigative symptoms whose function is the amassing of personal dossiers on tens of millions of Americans. This has become the method by which a large organisation makes judgments about people when it wants to hire or fire them, lend them money, or give them passports to travel abroad. A recent *Washington Post* survey noted that the largest American private investigative agency, the Retail Credit Company, which rates persons for a wide variety of purposes including industrial security, has 7,000 investigators, maintains dossiers on forty-two million people, and grosses more than $100 million annually from its activities. Credit Bureau Inc, the leading company in Washington, DC, maintains dossiers on 2.5 million present and former residents of the city. The Department of Defense has fourteen million life histories in its security files, the Civil Service eight million, and the FBI an unknown number (though it admits to some 100,000 on Communist 'sympathisers' alone). There are investigations and dossiers that people never ever learn about. For example, the Federal Housing Administration has private agencies conduct investigations of more than a million annual applicants for FHA loans. One purpose of these probes is to report on the 'marital stability' of applicants, based on the theory that there is more risk of foreclosure when divorce is threatening . . . Pending proposals and prospective developments of the next decade promise to raise even broader issues of privacy. For example, several study groups and a presidential task force have been working on proposals for a central federal data bank, to collect records of twenty federal agencies, such as Treasury, Labor, Commerce, Agriculture, and Health, Education and Welfare. These agencies already have 100 million punch cards and 30,000 computer tapes containing information about individuals and businesses. The data center would allow sharing of information within the federal government and access for other groups, such as business, research organisations, and state and local agencies. Material classified as confidential would not be given out, but what constitutes confidential material is far from clear and un-contested. Another computer facility under consideration by the federal government is a medical-data bank, holding tapes of the medical case histories of all Americans. Conceding its value for public-health purposes and for treating persons taken ill away from their home physicians, the question has already been raised as to who could press the button and get the medical print-out on an individual—his employer? a Congressional committee? the White House? Such a record would include such items as past mental or nervous problems, social diseases, sexual deviations, and the like, which could gravely compromise individuals if it came into the wrong hands. Another system recommended already by a federal study commission is a national, computerised job bank, with employment files on job seekers to match against job openings as these are reported in.

On top of this, there is the prospect of computer records of spending through the growing use of credit cards (some thinkers expect that cash will virtually be obsolete in another twenty years).

16B Alan F. Westin
MASTER FILES OF INDIVIDUAL LIVES

The life of the individual would be almost wholly recorded and observable through analysis of the daily 'transactions' of 'Credit Card No. 172,381,400, Humphrey, Stanley, M.' Who-ever ran the computers could know when the individual entered the highway and where he got off; how many bottles of Scotch or Vermouth he purchased from the liquor store; who paid the rent for the girl in Apartment 4B; who went to the movies between two and four P.M. on a working day at the office; who was at lunch at Luigi's or the Four Seasons on Tuesday, September 15; and the hotel at which Mrs. Smith spent the rainy afternoon last Sunday. Where every dollar came from that a government official banked, and where every dollar went that was spent by each corporation and labor union would also lie in the great treasury house of the computer. There would be few areas in which anyone could move about in the anonymity of personal privacy and few transactions that would not be fully documented for government examination.

Still another technological prospect is the collection, in various functional master memory systems, of basic information about each major aspect of the individual's life, an idea that has strong advocates in the governmental, scientific, and professional communities. The individual's complete educational record from pre-school nursery to post-graduate courses could be in the educational master file, including the results of all intelligence, aptitude, and personality tests taken during his lifetime. The individual's complete employment record could be in another master computer dossier.

This record would include every job held, rate of pay, efficiency ratings, employer evaluations, personality tests, recommendations, outside interests, family, relation to work, and so on, and would be available on instant print-out when the individual was being considered for new employment by a private organisation or government agency. The master credit file could contain all the information needed to do a thorough financial analysis of the individual: his income, fixed expenditures, pattern of past discretionary spending, savings, investment, predicted expenses based on personal and family history, and predicted promotion levels, and the like. Other central dossiers could deal with health, civic activity, telephone records and criminal records. Every person could have a personal identification number, and computer scanning of a cardholder's fingerprint or voice-print could control assumption of another's number or identity. . . . One small unit, containing one 4,800-foot reel of one-inch plastic tape, will be able to store in digital form about twenty pages of information (250 words of typing to the page) for every person in the United States, including women and children. Specific information from a person's twenty-page dossier on this reel could be retrieved in a maximum search time of four minutes, and the entire dossier could be printed out for dispatch to an inquiring source in a matter of a few more minutes.

SOURCE: Alan F. Westin. *Privacy and Freedom* (1970)

These information systems have also to be considered in connection with techniques of intrusion and surveillance. A French Government report noted in 1970:

17 UN Report
MAGNETIC CARD FILES

The development of increasingly sophisticated data processing techniques in the postal, telegraph and telecommunications service (PTT) has implications that have a bearing on the very general problem of the secrecy of magnetic card files.

Current research aims at replacing manual or mechanical sorting by automatic processes which will, on the basis of data processing, provide the postal service with card files on the domicile of users, individuals or companies, thereby facilitating certain operations such as home delivery, re-addressing and the maintenance of card files on companies. In addition, magnetic card files can be assembled rapidly for keeping the accounts of customers of the National Savings Bank and postal order, telephone and telex accounts.

As the postal services will have to keep such card files scrupulously up-to-date, it is quite likely that there will be interference between the service concerned and between them and other enterprises or administrative units.

The value of the PTT card files is already apparent and the results of their disclosure to other services can be imagined.

SOURCE: French Government communication to UN Commission on Human Rights, quoted in UN *Report* (E/CN4/1028, 1970)

18 Arthur R. Miller
PEN REGISTERS

A further significant threat to personal freedom is presented by the inevitable linking of computers to existing surveillance devices for monitoring people and their communications. One of the simplest of the present generation of snooping devices is the pen register, which, when attached to a telephone line, records on paper a series of dashes representing all numbers dialed from the selected telephone. But this snooping capability would be increased by several orders of magnitude if a few pen registers were attached to suspects' telephone lines and the information drawn in by these devices fed into a central computer. This technique could quickly provide a revealing analysis of patterns of acquaintances and dealings among a substantial group of people. Indeed this may be possible without pen registers; when the telephone companies' move to digital transmission is complete, a by-product may be a ready-made data base on past communications that waits only cross-correlation.

SOURCE: Arthur R. Miller. 'Personal Privacy in the Computer Age', *Michigan Law Review*, quoted in UN *Report* (E/CN4/1028, 1970)

In Britain, the Younger Report summed up the pace of development:

19 Younger Report
NUMBER OF COMPUTERS IN THE UK

According to Computer Survey for March/April 1971 the total number of computers in use or on order in the United Kingdom for all purposes in April 1971 was 6,075. A breakdown showing the areas in which they are used is given in Appendix M. It is

E

not possible to say exactly how many of these are relevant to our work, but, bearing in mind our terms of reference, our geographical remit (which excludes Northern Ireland) and those computers which have no implications for privacy, it seems likely that the total relevant number of computers is about 4,800. We arrive at this figure by subtracting from the total of 6,075 the number of computers in the hands of the armed services (344), local government (337), Government and other research establishments (238), public utilities (185), and Government Departments (149). We accept this figure as a very rough approximation which we could not confirm without lengthy investigation. As to future trends, one source estimated that total user expenditure on data processing in 1968 was £400m and was growing at the rate of about 25 per cent a year. The forward estimates of total expenditure for 1975 and 1980 were forecast at £1,400m and £2,100m.

SOURCE: *Report of the Committee on Privacy* (1972)

A report by Justice (the British section of the International Commission of Jurists) stresses:

20 Justice Report
RANGE OF COMPUTERISED INFORMATION

Until quite recently, the task of building up a coherent picture of someone else's private life without his consent has been one requiring so much time and effort as to deter all but the most determined. Regular physical surveillance; interviews with reluctant acquaintances, tradesmen, employers, landlords; painstaking research in public records and elsewhere; months, if not years, of single-minded effort were required to piece together the manner of a man's life from the traces which he leaves behind as he moves through his world.

With the advent of the electronic computer, all this information—and much more—can be made available in seconds to anyone who has access (lawfully or otherwise) to the right buttons and knows in what order to push them. A man's complete bank statements over many years will occupy a few feet of magnetic tape on one reel, his income tax returns a few inches on another, his hire-purchase acquisitions will be available on a third and his credit card transactions on a fourth. Within a few seconds, all these can be printed out for easy inspection, and between them they will not only give the clearest picture of every aspect of the subject's financial affairs, but will even show how many people he entertained at what restaurant on what day. Other segments of magnetic tape may hold all the details of his insurance policies and membership of associations, and as more and more organisations begin to use computers it will not be long before full records of his education, his driving convictions, his telephone calls, and eventually his political affiliations and his medical history, will be held on computer files. Once there, the right push on the right button will produce them in clear and legible form . . .

It therefore becomes economic to record a multitude of transactions which it was never before worth anyone's while to record at all, and possible for the first time to collate and edit this information. To take only two examples:

(a) It is likely to become economic in the foreseeable future for all hotels in a country to participate in a central computer-based reservation system. Once such a system is in operation, the touch of a button will throw up the information that, whenever Mr. X has spent a night at any hotel in the United Kingdom in the last two years, Miss Y has occupied the adjoining room. Without the computer this information might have been obtained— if at all—only at enormous cost in time and trouble.

(b) As we progress towards a cashless and chequeless society, more and more of our daily expenditure will be liquidated by the insertion of a personal plastic credit card into a wide variety of slots. It may not be long before this system becomes available for, say, supermarkets, public libraries, telephones and parking meters. In this way, the central system will acquire information, available at the touch of a button, about the tastes, interests and probable opinions and day-to-day whereabouts and contacts of any selected subject.

SOURCE: *Privacy and the Law, A Report by Justice* (1970)

It is technically feasible—though it has not yet happened anywhere—for all the information about individuals (medical, financial, and so forth) to be brought together in one large data-bank. Obviously this would wipe out one of the basic safeguards of privacy: that information should be seen only by those to whom it was given for a specific purpose—health details to the doctor or hospital, details of earnings to the tax inspector, etc.

21 Alan F. Westin
DATA BANKS

The intelligence [data bank] system is one in which decisions affecting the civil rights of the citizen as an individual will be made as a result of information supplied by the data bank. Examples would be the criminal justice information systems . . . that accumulate data for purposes of law enforcement, or personnel security, and loyalty data banks as these may develop . . . to collect information for purposes of personnel screening. The characteristic of such systems is that the files are organised according to each individual entered into the system, and the primary use of the files is to judge that individual in ways that would have a direct effect upon his civil rights.

Regulatory data banks in the governmental sector are those that are developing to deal with the economic, social, and welfare aspects of the citizen's life and would encompass government systems of data banks in the fields of education, welfare, health, business regulation, and the like. The data may be grouped according to classes of people but often the files are on an individual basis, and will be a major determinant of whether benefits and favours supplied or regulated by government are

available to a particular individual or the group or class to
which he belongs.

SOURCE: Paper prepared by Alan F. Westin for American
Civil Liberties Union, quoted in UN *Report* (E/CN4/1028,
1970)

22 Justice Report
DATA BANKS

A separate threat to privacy posed by the advent of the computer lies in the so-called 'data banks.' These should be thought
of not so much as computers, but as immense storage systems in
which an astronomic amount of information can be per-
manently held and extracted in any sequence, and in any
selected permutations, at any time. The usefulness of such
systems to the community is obvious, particularly in the fields
of medical statistics, planning, simulation of economic models,
prediction of demographic and other trends, and so forth. For
this reason, the US Federal Government has been anxious for
some years to establish a central data bank which would hold
'pertinent information' on all citizens of the United States, thus
greatly easing the task of the various federal departments and
agencies responsible for the government of the nation. So long
as the use of the data stored in the facility is confined to statistical purposes of this kind, the benefit is obvious. The danger
arises only because, by the very nature of the facility, it provides
an open invitation for the extraction of the full record of named
individuals, legitimately by those who have official access to the
facility, and possibly illegitimately by those who can obtain
access by fraud, stealth or corruption.

SOURCE: *Privacy and the Law, A Report by Justice* (1970)

*Of course, a great deal of information is collected for purposes which
have nothing to do with the individual. For instance, when an individual
is asked at a station where he is travelling to, the aim is to find out the*

total number of travellers on certain lines at certain times and improve the time-table. It may be asked, therefore, why the computer should store individual identities. But the fact is that this is always done.

23 Sawyer and Schechter
DATA CENTRES

Even though no scientific interest exists in examining the response of a single individual, it is necessary, in order to compute the over-all relation between, for example, income and education, to match an individual's income with his years of education.

The requirement for matching means that each individual record in the data centre must be identified, as by a social security number or, better (for guarding privacy), a special code number. Thus is it always theoretically possible to extract from a data centre information referring to a particular individual. This is true whether the centre is characterised as a 'statistical data centre' or as an 'intelligence or dossier file'.

Source: Sawyer and Schechter. 'Computers, Privacy and the National Data Centre', *American Psychologist* (Nov 1968), quoted in UN *Report* (E/CN4/1028, 1970)

From the privacy point of view, the most alarming fact about the computer is the ease with which information can be elicited from it. Professor Westin writes: 'Standardisation of computer languages and the perfection of machines that translate one machine language system into another have made it possible for computers to communicate directly with one another, so that data can flow in and out of separate systems.'

To get information from a computer, one needs to have either (a) another computer; or (b) a computer terminal, which is a much cheaper proposition; or (c) an ordinary telephone. This was explained at a recent conference called by the National Council of Civil Liberties:

24 NCCL conference
ACCESS TO COMPUTER INFORMATION

These modern systems constitute a vast communication network for digital information in which the central storage devices can be interrogated and the data processed with imper-
ceptible delays from many remote stations. By 'on-line' is meant
that communication is direct from the central processor to
peripheral equipment such as teletype consoles and visual display screens. The systems operate in 'real time', that is to say
the result of a processing operation is available instantly or on a
time-scale short compared to the process it is controlling or
monitoring. The term 'multi-access' indicates that the computer is available simultaneously to many users who may be at
terminals remote from the computer itself . . .

Real time computing means that many different people can
all 'converse' with a computer at the same time; thus the vast
speed and power of a computing system is broken down into
low powered units easily worked by ordinary people. This
technique allows the operators of the system to submit data
direct to the computer instead of through the medium of
forms, punched cards, paper tape and the like and so individuals can file information directly. Similarly, this means that
ordinary people can also access the files and edit and extract
information at the time they want it, and in the form they
want it.

In the computing industry this is a major advance as it re-
moves the costly, complex and confusing translation processes
and allows ordinary people directly to use computing power as
and when they want it. The various devices people use to
operate the computer do not have to be adjacent to the
machine as they can be connected over any distance through
Post Office telephone and telex circuits. To emphasise the
value and effect of this development one can see how it might
be used in the typical business where the salesman could enter

his day's sales on a terminal in his home, say in Exeter, the computer will check stocks and credit ratings, then print invoices in the firm's London office, the delivery note in the firm's warehouse in Bristol, re-schedule the factory and print out new instructions in the Midlands, and update the sales statistics on a television device in the head office in Edinburgh, all within seconds. This development also changes the whole structure of file access and file updating.

The most dramatic example is perhaps where the man pays with a credit card in a shop using a cash register that can read credit cards, connected to a computer. At the precise moment that a man makes a payment the computer knows precisely where the man is. Now every sensible computer planner will build in checks to stop a thief picking up a credit card in the street and using it. A simple loop in the program will allow lost card codes to be filed so that when a lost card is used some alarm is made at the cash register while another program loop could alert the nearest police station by a method similar to burglar alarm systems, so that the police could go and pick up the thief from the shop: the situation has changed out of all recognition. Today the credit card firm knows you went to that shop, but only days later. Lists of invalid credit card numbers are circulated and so a cashier might note a proffered card was invalid, but contacting the police could be difficult and obvious, which would alert the thief. One could argue that this system could only do good reducing frauds on shops, etc., but if the use of such a system was widespread it does not require a great stretch of the imagination to work out how a totalitarian government could turn the situation to its advantage.

The logic of computing would suggest that as computers think in numbers more easily than the alphabet it would be far more straightforward for computers to identify each member of the community by a code number suitably chosen to be unique, and it would further seem rational to use the same code for all purposes—indeed for every computer service to identify one single person by a different code would seem to be quite stupid.

However, such a simple decision would, of course, offer a standard access code to every file. Thus once a person had quite legitimately used someone else's code in one environment, that person would have the means of access and obtain every fact about the other.

The ability to link up many users to one computer would indicate that perhaps the whole of one national operation—health records—should be run on one very large network of machines. Indeed the ability of a hospital at Luton to access the medical record of a casualty brought in from the M1 and discover he had received certain drugs prescribed by his doctor in Manchester the day before, might save that injured person's life. However, to provide such a wonderful system would mean, by definition, that a very large number of people indeed would always have access to all the facts about every person's health.

SOURCE: B. C. Rowe (ed). *Privacy, Computers and You* (National Computing Centre, 1972)

The impersonality of the computer—the fact that it cannot think, but can only collate and reproduce the 'bits' of information submitted to it— creates dangers in many spheres.

25 Arthur R. Miller
DAMAGING AND DISTORTED INFORMATION

Contextual errors can occur in a number of ways. Raw, un-evaluated data about an individual, especially when recorded in a cryptic fashion, might give rise to damaging inferences that a fuller explication of the underlying events, direct knowledge of the information's source, or professional analysis of the facts would show to be false. Illustrative of this type of distortion is a terse entry stating that an individual was arrested, convicted of a felony, and sentenced to a federal penitentiary for a certain number of years. Undoubtedly data of this description would detrimentally affect the subject's ability to obtain employment or credit. Yet our 'felon' may simply have been a conscientious objector who could not meet the requirements for exemption from military service on the grounds of religious belief that existed at the time he refused to be inducted.

Taken at face value, this kind of entry is doubly dangerous if the events occurred in the distant past and the legal or social attitude toward the particular 'offense' has changed with the passage of time. Consider the potential effect of the following computer profile: 'Arrested, June 1, 1962; disorderly conduct and criminal conspiracy; convicted, April 12, 1963; sentenced, May 21, 1963, six months.' Without more, how would a person viewing the entry know that what appears to be an anti-social type is merely a civil rights activist who spent some of his time during the early sixties working for the desegregation of educational facilities in the South or for equal employment opportunities for ghetto blacks in the North? And what about the conviction? Perhaps it merely reflects the now-discredited judicial and law enforcement practices of a decade ago of inhibiting the exercise of constitutionally protected rights of free speech and public assembly by invoking disorderly conduct, trespass, and conspiracy ordinances against what often were peaceful protests seeking racial and social justice. Indeed, the 'conviction' may even have been reversed on appeal and our 'offender' exonerated . . .

What is potentially far more dangerous is that many information gatherers fail to recognise the necessity of entering supplemental data to reduce the damaging effect of an earlier entry that has derogatory overtones. To return to the subject of arrest records, police departments throughout the nation can obtain an FBI 'rap sheet' containing a suspect's criminal record by sending his fingerprints to Washington. These sheets are supposed to include information on any court proceeding that might follow each arrest, but these data apparently are not furnished in approximately thirty-five percent of the cases. Often, failures to prosecute and acquittals are not indicated. Despite an even more distressing situation on the state and

local level, many of the emerging computerised law enforcement information systems are making their files more widely
available without undertaking any substantial effort to make
them more accurate.

The significance of arrest records is brought home by the
application of a recently enacted New York statute that requires the fingerprinting of brokerage house employees. Early
in 1970, a number of workers were discharged by brokerage
firms on the basis of their past 'records,' which in some cases
merely indicated that the employee had been arrested. One can
only hope that the discharges were based on something more
than an unexplicated entry on file with the New York's Identification and Intelligence System. But since the employee is not
permitted to see the 'rap sheet' on him and has either no right
of appeal or an extremely limited one, we probably will never
know what actually happened.

In an era of great social activism on the part of the young
with counterpoint demands from others for 'Law and Order,'
arrests are bound to increase. But many of them will be of a
strikingly different character than what has been typical in the
past. It is now common for hundreds of college demonstrators
or black militants to be arrested in connection with one incident. Using recent experience as a guide, only a small fraction
of the group will be prosecuted, and an even smaller number
convicted. All of them, however, will have arrest records. The
problem is particularly grave for our black citizens. In the past,
many police forces, North and South, have been quite cavalier
about taking blacks into custody, which means that a dis-
proportionately high percentage have 'arrest' (but not necessarily conviction) records.

SOURCE: Arthur R. Miller. *The Assault on Privacy* (1972)

*At a conference called by the National Council for Civil Liberties a
psychologist said:*

26A NCCL conference
STORAGE AND INTERPRETATION OF PSYCHIATRIC DATA

Although psychologists apply their expertise in three main areas, namely the educational, clinical and occupational fields, there are certain features common to all three and these will be discussed first. There is, for example, the importance of trust. Unless the subject believes that what he reveals about himself to the psychologist is reasonably confidential he will suppress important facts, thus making the psychologist's task very difficult. 'Reasonably confidential' is, of course, a vague term and must be defined, preferably by the subject himself, and accepted by the psychologist. If a mutually acceptable definition of confidentiality cannot be arrived at it may be impossible for the psychologist to perform his duties with respect to that particular subject. However, in most circumstances there is little or no difficulty on this score. Some specific details of attitudes or behaviour, e.g. answers to a standardised personality inventory, may be absolutely confidential, i.e. they will not be revealed by the psychologist to anyone else and need not be stored anywhere. Interestingly enough, with the advent of computerised scoring and automated testing, the answers need not be revealed even to the psychologist as it is often possible to process electronically the subject's written replies to arrive at a relevant score without the psychologist wishing to know the answer to any specific question.

Since, however, the psychologist is usually working as a member of a team he would expect to be able to pass on information obtained about the subject or from the subject to the other members of that team. This information might be included in a data bank as long as access was confined to the members of the team, e.g. in the psychiatric field to those psychiatrists, psychologists and social workers who are actively working on the particular case. Some of the information of the team might be passed on to a larger group within the same organisation. For example, in the same context, the diagnosis, treatment and prognosis arrived at by the psychiatric group might go into the hospital case record or the NHS general medical record of the patient, with access available to a larger NHS group and in particular to the patient's own general practitioner. It is therefore essential that the computer experts incorporate into any institution's data bank a system of safe-guarding different levels of confidentiality.

Another problem in all fields of applied psychology arises from the distinction between the raw data, e.g. replies by the subject to specific questions on an inventory, and the conclusions drawn by the psychologist from the answers to a number of such questions. Firstly, the psychologist would not regard the answer to a single question as being very significant and in most inventories scale scores are arrived at by summing the answers to several related questions. Secondly, he would interpret those sub-scale scores on the basis of scores obtained by a representative group of individuals comparable to the subject in all important variables and, finally, he would draw conclusions in the light of everything else he knew about the subject and the circumstances under which the inventory had been completed. For example, the applicant for a job might be expected to have portrayed himself in the most favourable light, while the depressed patient may be pathologically self-critical. Because of this need for interpretation of much of his raw data, the psychologist will always tend to be chary about making it available to those who lack the skill and training to interpret it validly. It is likely, therefore, that he will wish to make his basic raw data available only to other psychologists and even standardised scores, such as IQ, available only when accompanied by his interpretation of their meaning, so that, for example, the IQ obtained in a test would not be given even to anyone entitled to have it without the statement by the psychologist as to how far it is likely to be a fair estimate of the subject's true level of intelligence.

All entries in a data bank should include the identity of the person who has inserted that information so that responsibility can be allocated to the appropriate person and action taken in cases of false or culpably erroneous insertions. The conscientious psychologist would have nothing to fear from this reasonable safeguard.

To turn now to each of the applied fields, there is first of all the educational psychologist. Few children manage to complete their schooling nowadays without undergoing at least one intelligence test and several standardised attainment tests. Some will also be seen in the child guidance clinic because of problems which may vary from educational backwardness to delinquency, along with a large contingent of enuretics and school refusers. For these disturbed children information will be collected and stored not only about the child himself but also about his family, including the child's view of his parents and his parents' views of him, emphasising that a psychologist's data consists not only of facts but also of opinions. As in the general case the trust between psychologist and client will only be maintained if this information is available only to the team involved in the child's case. Information of a more formal type, e.g. IQ and measured level of attainment could be stored in education officers' files as long as their limited value was stressed, so that an IQ of eighty at the age of eight, tested when the child was in an emotionally disturbed state, would not brand that child as a dullard for the rest of his life.

Psychologists who work in hospitals will share with their medical and nursing colleagues the problems of medical records, but psychiatry has its own special problems in this respect. Firstly, in investigating the emotional difficulties of the patient more intimate information must often be elicited than is necessary in other medical specialities. This information is sometimes highly interesting to an employer or to a wife but it must not be given to them without the patient's explicit permission. Secondly, the fact that many psychiatric patients are out of touch with reality means that their statements cannot be taken as factual. When the otherwise healthy sailor informs the venereologist that he suspects he has venereal disease it is usually an admission that he has had illicit intercourse at some time or other, but the depressed patient who informs the psychiatrist that she has venereal disease may always have lived an absolutely chaste life. Finally, in some forms of psychotherapy, in particular Freudian psychoanalysis, the patient is encouraged to voice his phantasies which may be of a very primitive kind, symbolic and unintegrated, rather than a conscious point of view, and these should never go into public records.

In general, many details in the psychiatric case record are seldom relevant outside the psychiatric situation and it is doubtful if they should be generally available to other medical departments. For these reasons many psychiatric departments in general hospitals already maintain a separate system of case records for psychiatry, so that when the patient is seen in another department of the hospital his psychiatric case notes are not available to that department. In a data bank similar safeguards would appear to be important so that the psychiatric information about a patient should not be automatically supplied to an enquirer even within the medical profession, or to lawyers. This would ensure that only a psychologist or psychiatrist as appropriate would have access to psychiatric material, although either would supply a report based on that material to anyone who had a right to it. With such safeguards it would not appear unreasonable to maintain data banks of medical and psychiatric information on patients.

At the same conference, doctors made important points:

26B NCCL conference
STORING MEDICAL HISTORIES

We in the hospital service have gone forward from the punch card era of computers to data banks. We have already used record linkage to identify individuals treated in various hospitals and in general practices, in order to have more information about their medical histories. Thus we have created data banks. We are also, on the administrative side of the hospital service, to use computers in hospital activity analysis, that is, analysing a small amount of data about patients collectively and not individually, offering management information in relation to patients' stay and in relation to the cost of disease. This information bank already exists and is being used for patient medical management. We are only in the early days of computers and we have not yet, in Britain, manipulated large data banks, although this is on the horizon and plans are now being cast for these.

In the computer system we are designing at King's College Hospital, the main objective is for a total patient record. The record will embody not only hospital but general practitioner data of various kinds. This will be the start of a data bank. Once the hurdle of dealing with medical information is crossed, which is going to happen in the foreseeable future, then data banks in the medical services will become a reality. It is hoped in the Health Service that most of the difficulties can be dealt with by rules at the local hospital level—this will involve all the issues of confidentiality. We must not forget, however, that many of these are unwritten and rely on the 'good sense' of people. The civil service and the National Health Service also have a series of rules for dealing with confidentiality and we have relied on these to date. However, in the telecommunications era or the electronic era which is about to begin, no longer can we trust entirely to the good sense of individuals. We have to specify the means in detail and this often requires us to get down to the most idiotic details . . .

At present there are the professional people who can access a patient's record at any time and he has no say over this. He does not even know that it goes on. He is informed when he has to give consent for it to go outside. Unfortunately, one has to admit that he often is not aware of the depth and wide-reaching nature of its content when permission is given, and usually assumes that it is a doctor-to-doctor transaction and that there will be some professional monitoring at either end.

In future, we have to design many more safeguards into the system specifically. I think the patient has a right certainly on request, probably at the payment of a fee (because everything costs money) to find out who has accessed his record and why. I think the reason as well as the access ought to be recorded. It is already implicit within our system that whoever accessed the information is known as well as the time of entry. Many deductions can be made from even those two simple bits of information.

Furthermore, there ought to be a right—and this is a much more controversial problem which needs much more discussion —for an individual to have his record deleted from the system. In other words, he ought to have a right of deletion as well as a right of completion and entry. This is a much more difficult issue from the point of view of the individual's rights and freedom, whether he has a right to opt out of the system, and say, 'Thank you very much, I have had my treatment. That was an episode. Now I demand to be deleted.' It may not be acceptable for the health service to have total deletion—perhaps there may be certain information about blood groups, etc., that ought to be retained. But we should have a right to delete some of the data which may exist . . .

We have talked about medical data banks. The sort of thing that frightens me is to be found in the Thamesmead experimental data bank. I have been through the categories of information to be recorded. I shall just give you one little block of it, so you will understand what people are up to, and hoping to rely on. This collection is headed 'demographic data' and includes marital status, dependancy on head of household, all occupations and dates if possible, economic activity according to Registrar General's classification, social class according to occupation of head of household—already we are in contentious areas—type of dwelling, number of persons in house, smoking habits, alcohol consumption and social episodes (plain

F

language insertions put in by social workers). This is a communal medical data bank which will be accessed by the doctors. It is difficult to cope with this stuff when it is written down on paper—what is going to happen when we start putting it up on computer systems and try to rely on it?

SOURCE: B. C. Rowe (ed). *Privacy, Computers and You* (National Computing Centre, 1972)

Then there is the question of computer mistakes. Strictly speaking, computers do not make mistakes; the mistakes are made by the programmers who feed in information. What computers cannot do is to recognise these mistakes. The consequences can be serious, as in an example cited by Mr Harvey Matusow:

27 Harvey Matusow
THE COMPUTER'S INABILITY
TO RECOGNISE MISTAKES

A case in point happened a few months ago to a friend of mine —an executive for a large American TV Network. He received his monthly statement from a company with whom he had a credit card and it was for twice the amount of his purchases for that month. The itemised account was correct, but when totalling, the computer had doubled the amount.

He checked it against his own receipts, which he had kept very meticulously, and discovered that, yes, the computer had made a mistake.

He wrote a polite letter to the company, enclosing a cheque for the correct amount (half of that demanded in the invoice) and explained what had obviously happened. He received a letter back, thanking him, and saying it would be corrected.

Three weeks later he received a reminder: 'PLEASE PAY THE BALANCE'. He photostated the correspondence—sent it back to the credit company, asking them to please see to the matter.

Shortly after, he received another letter which demanded the return of his credit card, and telling him that his credit had been cancelled.

At that point he made a visit to the credit company, only to be told that there was nothing that could be done, because the computer had been programmed to reject his name and credit card number.

'I understand,' he said. 'It's difficult to make corrections in computers. Why don't you give me another card with a different number?'

'But we can't do that,' he was told, 'because the computer has been programmed to reject your name and social security number also. And furthermore, we are sorry, but our computer is connected to other credit computers and it has fed them information stating that you're a bad credit risk.'

Sure enough, within a few weeks, he received letters from three other companies with whom he had credit, demanding the return of their cards, all of which had been cancelled.

The computer had made a judgment decision by not checking with any operator before transmitting the false information.

SOURCE: B. C. Rowe (ed). *Privacy, Computers and You* (National Computing Centre, 1972)

In Britain, both computer-users (in general) and computer manufacturers have shown themselves aware of the problem of privacy and willing to accept safeguards. The conference called by the National Council of Civil Liberties and reported in the book Privacy, Computers and You, *was willingly attended by representatives of the computer industry. Certain safeguards for privacy are perfectly feasible, as one of them explained:*

28 NCCL conference
COMPUTER SECURITY SYSTEMS

As the information enters the file, its origin, degree of confidentiality and destination within the file can be logged. Within the computer it is possible to hold all or parts of the information in sealed compartments, and to scramble it within these compartments. As it leaves the computer the content, time and name of the user can be logged. A system operating like the passkeys to a vault permits the imposing of any rules and safeguards an organisation may wish.

Facilities for implementing these safeguards are now included in the various program packages offered by computer manufacturers. The way they are implemented is the private concern of the user, but the facility is there.

How secure can these arrangements be? We have yet to devise a code that cannot be broken, and it is true that, even if it is harder to gain access to computer files, the concentration of information within them could make it more worthwhile to try. But the facts to remember are these. First, computerised information is held in a form that restricts access to those who are acquainted intimately both with computer systems in general and the system in question. Next, the imposition of monitoring and passkey techniques means that any betrayal of security needs the connivance of as many executives as one cares to nominate. Thirdly, the 'passkeys' can be changed more frequently than any physical key. And, finally, the logging of entries and withdrawals of information is automatic. The combination of connivance and technical skills needed to break into data banks is therefore considerably greater than those needed for entering ordinary filing systems.

Source: B. C. Rowe (ed). *Privacy, Computers and You* (National Computing Centre, 1972)

The Younger Committee also tackled this problem and recommended built-in safeguards to prevent easy access to computerised information and undesirable disclosure:

29A Younger Report
SECURITY SAFEGUARDS FOR COMPUTERISED INFORMATION

Unauthorised access could occur inside a central computer installation; where it involved circumvention of security devices it would usually require collusion on the part of those working the installation. Outside an installation it could occur during information preparation, handling of printout or transmission to terminals. To the extent that breaches of security measures could occur only where there was sufficient collusion among the staff of the installation involved, computers are neither more nor less vulnerable than older systems. The fear of many of those outside the computer world who have given evidence relates mainly to access from terminals. In this connection it is important to bear in mind that links with terminals may be by private or public telephone lines or short wave radio. Access from terminals can be controlled by simply locking the terminal or the room containing it; by restricting access to sensitive information in the main computer store to specified terminals; by providing terminal-users with individual identity codes (such as keys, badges or tokens inserted at the terminal) or passwords which must accompany a request for information; by requiring an authorised terminal-user to answer random questions about his background to which only he will know the answers; or by voice identification techniques (still at an early stage of development). In addition it is possible for a computer to be programmed to produce periodically a statement of the information it has supplied to each terminal, so that its activity can be monitored.

Devices of this kind, however, are very far from allaying all the anxieties which arise from the increasingly widespread use of the computer. It must be borne in mind that computer technology is already a massive industry employing thousands of people. These employees are being recruited at high speed and without any great degree of discrimination, because there is a constant unsatisfied demand for new staff. They are rapidly trained; advertisements on London Underground platforms tell us that it is possible to qualify as a computer programmer after a course lasting no more than six weeks. There is no long-standing tradition of discretion and responsibility, comparable—for instance—to the traditions of the medical profession. In the nature of things, it seems inevitable that some among the many thousands of computer employees will be indifferent to considerations of privacy; some will regard safeguards of confidentiality as a mere nuisance involving extra work, to be ignored whenever it is safe; and a few will be open to bribes and inducements, or willing to make unauthorised disclosures because they see this as a trivial matter. The atmosphere of computer work accentuates the dangers; the stress is placed on speed and convenience, and the highest value is placed on meeting the requirements of customers and providing a 'full service'.

The Younger Committee showed itself aware—though, in the opinion of some observers, not sufficiently aware—of these inherent problems. It came up with a series of remedies which amount to a kind of privacy charter:

29B Younger Report
RECOMMENDATIONS ON COMPUTER
PROCEDURE

There could be an incentive to cover the cost of the acquisition and recording of information by using it for purposes additional to that for which it was originally collected. For example a computerised record of subscribers to a trade publication might well prove useful to the manufacturers of certain products advertised therein. The situation could be a clear breach of privacy in so far as it could be held that private information (a name and address) given solely for the purpose of receiving a magazine is passed on without the authority of the originator. Therefore:

1. Information should be regarded as held for a specific purpose and not be used, without appropriate authorisation, for other purposes; and
2. Access to information should be confined to those authorised to have it for the purpose for which it was supplied.

Furthermore, because it is often cheaper to collect all available information in one operation and because computers have the capacity to store it, there could be a double incentive for the owners of computers to hoard large amounts of information some of which, though not essential now, might prove useful at some later date. We believe that:

3. The amount of information collected and held should be the minimum necessary for the achievement of the specified purpose.

A great deal of personal information is acquired to provide statistics to assist planning and other research, or is acquired for some other purpose and subsequently adapted to a form suitable for such ends. Planners and researchers, however, rarely need to know identities of individuals. Therefore:

4. In computerised systems handling information for statistical purposes, adequate provision should be made in their design and programs for separating identities from the rest of the data.

We discuss later in this chapter the arguments for and against supplying individuals with a copy of the information held about them in a computerised record. While we do not believe that a printout should automatically be supplied, we think that every system should be so designed that in situations where printout is appropriate an individual can on request be told of the contents of the record. Therefore:

5. There should be arrangements whereby the subject could be told about the information held concerning him.

We are not convinced that considerations of privacy are at present sufficiently in the minds of computer users and we think that more regard should be paid to such considerations than is the case now. Therefore:

6. The level of security to be achieved by a system should be specified in advance by the user and should include precautions against the deliberate abuse or misuse of information.

Most of the security measures we have discussed earlier in this chapter have been preventive. A security system would be incomplete, however, if it did not include provision for the detection of an irregularity. Therefore:

7. A monitoring system should be provided to facilitate the detection of any violation of the security system.

There are three further principles of only marginal relevance to privacy, which we feel we should put forward for consideration alongside the seven we enumerate above. Computers have the capacity to retain information in effect indefinitely so that it is occasionally stored, in the form of discs or tapes, with little regard to a time limit. Therefore:

8. In the design of information systems, periods should be specified beyond which the information should not be retained.

Private sector computer users usually have a commercial interest in ensuring the accuracy and up-to-dateness of information and protecting it against corruption during processing. There are at present, however, no procedures in general use for dealing quickly with inaccuracies. Therefore:

9. Data held should be accurate. There should be machinery for the correction of inaccuracy and the updating of information.

The coding of subjective judgments often entails the loss of shades of meaning and emphasis. For example, a numeral indicating 'fair' in evaluating an employee's performance is capable of wide interpretation. In such cases it would be preferable to refer the interrogator of the computer to a more detailed report. Therefore:

   10. Care should be taken in coding value judgments.

SOURCE: *Report of the Committee on Privacy* (1972)

Nevertheless, the Committee was forced to conclude that no safeguards can provide against all conceivable eventualities. Lapses are bound to occur, simply because this field of technology is new, experimental and constantly developing; and also because the safeguarding of privacy has never been a major consideration. The warning has been reinforced with considerable frankness by a spokesman for the British Computer Society:

30 British Computer Society
LACK OF RELIABILITY IN COMPUTER SERVICE

It is not sufficiently appreciated that there is no known method of fully checking out (i.e. removing *all* the logical errors in) a substantial computer program. Yet the size, number and complexity of these programs is steadily increasing. This especially applies in the large-scale installations, handling hundreds or thousands of connected terminals, which will have the greatest impact on the public. The position in these installations can be contrasted with that of the telephone system.

   The public is often critical of the GPO because some of their calls may be cut off or a given terminal (e.g. your particular telephone) may be inoperative. However, as a system the telephone service is remarkable. It never fails as a whole and very rarely at the level of a local exchange. By comparison, computing systems are far too prone to collapse entirely. We just do not, as yet, have the programming ability to ensure a similar reliability of service, in very large projects, as that commonly attained in telecommunications. This is now a subject of enormous technical concern. Some progress is being made, but slowly. There is little relevant research and the problems involved have been seriously under-estimated by management in both business and government.

Despite the obvious risks which arise from this lack of reliability there are no mandatory, or even commonly accepted, safeguards which are applied to systems affecting the public welfare. Computers are already used to monitor conditions in nuclear power stations, to help control the distribution of electricity in the national grid and to pay innumerable pensions. No doubt the bodies concerned have behaved with complete responsibility. But the public does not know who has exercised what safeguards . . .

SOURCE: B. C. Rowe (ed). *Privacy, Computers and You* (National Computing Centre, 1972)

It must be borne in mind, too, that it is much easier to build safeguards into computers when they are installed than to add the safeguards after installation. It has been reckoned that the former job adds 5 per cent to the cost, and the latter job 25 per cent. Unfortunately, many 'first-generation' computers are in use and awareness of the privacy problem was not developed for some time:

31 UN Report
CONTROL OF ACCESS TO DATA BANK INFORMATION

Mechanical or technical means of controlling access to data-bank information have been developed and used primarily in connexion with time-sharing systems, i.e., the fast-growing system of renting time for the use of a single large computer to several independent users. As recently as 1966, however, methods of enhancing the privacy of data in a time-sharing system were considered to be 'a very poorly studied problem . . . There is practically nothing to be found in the computer literature on the subject.' While awareness of the problem has grown since then, only recently has a working system with more than password protection been developed. 'In nearly all systems to date, a user's password will get him into his file directory and into any file referenced in that directory.' In such systems information is safe only to the extent that knowledge of the password is limited; this is not a very reliable safeguard in the light of sophisticated eavesdropping and other surveillance techniques. Furthermore, a password system provides only a single barrier at the entrance to the entire filing system, the contents of which may be very broad in scope. For instance, there is no provision for discriminating between 'sensitive' information about an individual, which should be protected against access by certain users, and other information.

SOURCE: UN *Report* (E/CN4/1028, 1970). The quotations are from papers published in the United States.

PART TWO

The Power of the State

POLICE RECORDS

In its most visible sense, the power of the State over the citizen is embodied in the police force. Many aspects of police work—inquiry, detection, pursuit and arrest—obviously cannot be carried out without intrusion on privacy, and the concern of society is to strike a balance between the disadvantages of this intrusion and the advantage of security against crime. The power of search is emphatically a case in point, and the balance has been struck by the long-standing rule that a search requires a magistrate's warrant. This rule has recently been breached by the Dangerous Drugs Act, 1970, which empowers police officers to search persons and private premises without a warrant when they suspect the possession of illegal drugs.

Even before this Act had been passed, however, searches for drugs had caused some resentment—for example, when a pub in Torbay was raided (with a warrant) and about seventy people were made to strip, completely or to their underwear. According to the statements made, 'this meant a highly personal and embarrassing search of their bodies' and 'there was no serious effort made to ensure complete privacy of the sexes'. The search lasted for two hours, and 'everyone was questioned intensively about their movements, their friends and their activities'. A petition of protest was signed by 150 people describing themselves as regular customers of the pub.

Representations from the National Council for Civil Liberties brought the following reply from the Assistant Chief Constable of the Devon and Cornwall Constabulary:

32 Assistant Chief Constable, Devon and Cornwall Constabulary
REPLY TO A PETITION OF PROTEST

A thorough investigation into the complaints made in the petition has been carried out and the Chief Constable is satisfied that the matters referred to in the petition are without foundation . . . In the course of the investigation it was ascertained that Mr Thomas Clifford Watthey, who describes himself as the Secretary of the Torbay Rights Association and resides at 5 Coburg Place, Torquay, was the person responsible for the preparation and circulation of the petition.

SOURCE: *The Police and the Citizen*, NCCL pamphlet (1969)

To be convicted of possessing illegal drugs—or of any other crime—is to acquire a criminal record. In the light of Professor Miller's remarks (25), this question of records is worthy of reflection in the context of privacy. In Britain, records are maintained locally by the various county police forces, and on a national basis by the Criminal Records Office at the headquarters of the Metropolitan Police (New Scotland Yard). A full study has been made by Mr James B. Rule.

Incidentally, while Mr Rule was preparing his book for publication, he was asked by a Home Office official to supply a copy of his chapter on police records 'so that we can read it and if appropriate comment on it before it goes to a publisher'. After a lapse of over two months, the comment from Sir Philip Allen took this form: 'There is so much in the chapter—in content, in emphasis and in your speculative paragraphs— with which I disagree that it would be possible to meet my points only by leaving out substantial passages and making fundamental changes in others'.

Mr Rule gives the following description of the filing system in the Criminal Records Office:

33A James B. Rule
CRIMINAL RECORDS OFFICE FILING SYSTEM

These files make up the most voluminous and discursive, and in many ways the most important, records kept by the police. Their maintenance is probably also the task requiring the greatest expenditure of resources, in terms of staff time and amount of space. Entered in large manila folders, filed numerically according to the sequence of their creation, and shelved very nearly from floor to ceiling in row after row of racks, they give the distinct impression of the stacks of a closed-access library. Continuously plying these stacks are the staff of civil servants of the clerical grades. Like their counterparts in a library, they receive a constant flow of slips requesting specific files for use outside at the 'Main Desk', and an equally predictable flow of used files to be returned to their correct places. Circling around and through the stacks is a system of trolleys, which move the files from the stacks to their destinations and return used files, and requests for new ones, to the staff.

The fact that the files are organised by number rather than by name makes it necessary to keep a nominal index, to link the one with the other. This nominal index serves the same purpose as a library card catalogue. It consists of small slips, filed in loose-leaf binders according to the surname of the criminal. These list the criminal's full name, any aliases or variants of his name, his date of birth, and his 'CRO Number', representing the key to the location of his file within the 'stacks'. At the beginning of 1971, there were approximately 3,000,000 entries in the nominal index at New Scotland Yard, a number considerably exceeding the total of 2,500,000 criminal records. The discrepancy stems from the fact that many of those whose files appear have also passed through the system under different names, all of which must be linked to the single criminal record file.

What of the contents of the files? They consist mainly of

three documents found in nearly every file, plus a few others occurring much more rarely . . . The first of the three is a sheet itself called the 'criminal record' file. The 'criminal record' in this narrowest sense is the straightforward listing of the individual's criminal career, conviction by conviction, from the first to the most recent. It notes the courts, the sentences, the offences for which the convictions took place, and the dates, along with the name and CRO number of the criminal.

The second of the three main documents making up the criminal record is what is often termed the 'descriptive form', or more simply the 'DF'. This detailed data-sheet is made up for every occasion when charges are brought against a man, and retained in the files every time there is a conviction. It gives a complete description of the individual, the circumstances of the arrest, the arresting officer and police force, as well as his name, his current address and the date. It will also include a photograph in all but a very small minority of cases. The most recent example of this form will thus provide the police with useful information about the criminal, should they want to locate him at some time subsequent to his last listed conviction.

The third main document contained in the criminal record folder, unlike the other two, is not made out according to any set form. This 'antecedent history' sheet is always in discursive prose. In the event of a defendant's conviction, the courts require presentation of a statement from the police concerning his background and circumstances. This is in addition to the listing of his past convictions, which the courts also require. The contents of the antecedent history sheets vary considerably, according to the habits of the police force and the requirements of the courts, but certain inclusions are standard. It will almost always provide some description of the defendant's family life and place of residence. Equally predictable are some mentions of his employment history, financial situation, and customary associates. The original purpose of this sheet was to aid the court in setting an appropriate and reasonable sentence for the crime, but it is also a matter of routine to file copies of it in the criminal record. Like the descriptive form, this sheet can be useful in subsequent attempts by the police to contact the individual.

. . . Like other systems of mass surveillance, police record-keeping works to associate people with their past behaviour. More than many of its counterparts, however, this system often faces especially energetic efforts from its clientele to forestall this association. The work of the police in this respect would be all but impossible except that every person's fingerprints are unchanging and unique, and that fingerprints are subject to classification and indexing, so that single prints can be matched or places systematically within even large collections. Police identification procedures are predicated on these facts, with the result that criminal record offices, both in London and in the provinces, work in the closest cooperation within their associated fingerprint offices. The pattern of this partnership is highly predictable. The Criminal Record Office compiles details of crimes and criminal records, while the fingerprint staff specialise in linking both crimes and criminal records to specific persons. Thus the establishment of positive identification is virtually the whole of the task of the Fingerprint Office. Like the Criminal Record Office itself, this office organises its activities around a series of different files:

The Nominal Index. Like the Criminal Record Office, the Fingerprint Office of the Metropolitan Police relies upon a small file to link people's names to the file locations of their finger-prints. Here, too, the nominal index consists of small slips filed according to surname. Each slip also lists any variants or aliases of the person's name, the Criminal Record Office number, and the classification number corresponding to the set of ten fingerprints.

The 'Mains' Collection. This is the core of the fingerprint collection, corresponding roughly to the criminal record files in the Criminal Record Office. For the great majority of criminal record files there should be an entry in this collection, consist-ing of a full set of ten fingerprints taken by the police. On 1

January 1971, there were approximately 2,154,000 of these sets on file. Each set is arrayed on a large, loose-leaf sheet, much like those used in photo albums, filed according to the classification in which the set belongs, and bound with other prints belonging to the same classification. Besides the full set of prints, each sheet also contains the individual's name and CRO number.

The 'Singles' File. There are many occasions when the Fingerprint Office must check an incoming print to determine whether it matches any print in their collections, without knowing whose print it is or which finger it comes from. For these and other purposes, it is necessary to maintain a file of fingerprints contained in the 'Mains' collection, with each individual print filed separately according to its fingerprint classification. This index does not comprise all prints contained in the 'Mains' collection, however, but only those of persons convicted of breaking offences, motor vehicle theft, and crimes of violence. The classification system used by the police merely allows the assignment of each fingerprint to a category, without locating it within that category. Thus, searching for fingerprints from well-represented categories in this index takes much longer than for prints from rare groupings . . .

The Wanted and Missing Persons Index

This index, maintained by the Criminal Record Office, is considerably less complex in its organisation and contents than the criminal records. Basically, it is a comprehensive, central listing of persons wanted for arrest, detention or questioning by the police and other agencies throughout Britain. It is of special interest for this study in that it enables the police to extend the net of their surveillance to apprehend persons well outside the locales in which they are wanted. It consists of a large number of small file cards—numbering approximately 65,000 at the beginning of 1971—filed alphabetically by surname of wanted person, listing for each a brief description, date of birth, the agency by which the person is wanted, and the circumstances

G

under which they are sought. Located next to the array of twenty telephones used for this purpose, the index is constantly under interrogation, as police from both London and the provinces check the status of persons they encounter in the course of their work. It is the never-ending flow of inquiries to this index which requires around-the-clock staffing of the Metropolitan Criminal Record Office.

Mr Rule next describes the way in which the police are able to make use of their records:

33B James B. Rule
POLICE USE OF CRO INFORMATION

It is impossible to understand the workings of police record-keeping without first considering the several broad categories of inquiries which make up the bulk of its business. Perhaps the most important of these is the 'stop check', in which the police-man on his beat checks the names of persons he encounters against listings in the regional or national criminal record office. Such inquiries are part of the basic routine of policing, learned as such by all policemen in the course of their training. Thus, whenever a policeman on patrol encounters someone who, by appearance, manner, whereabouts or whatever, appears suspect, he is apt to detain him long enough to check his status with the nearest criminal record office. In most parts of Britain, the constable has no legal power to hold any person against his wishes without arrest, although it is safe to assume that the police do not emphasise these facts to those whom they accost. In any case, most Britons submit to these procedures without much fuss, to such an extent that anyone who refuses such an inquiry is apt by so doing to subject himself to still further attention.

At one time, it was necessary for the policeman making the inquiry to locate a telephone box and to place his inquiry from there to the nearest criminal record office. Now, however, most 'stop checks' are entered initially from the small personal radios which virtually all patrolling policemen carry, or from police auto radios. Such inquiries go to the nearest police radio receiver, and from there are relayed to the nearest criminal record office; the response is then relayed back to the inquiring policeman. The result, for the criminal record offices, is a constant flow of telephone inquiries, and a considerable investment of resources in processing such inquiries. The Metropolitan Criminal Record Office maintains a battery of twenty telephones for such inquiries, ten apiece for requests from London and from the provinces. The typical regional office has four or five telephone lines for such requests, and both the Metropolitan and some regional offices are equipped to answer inquiries directly by radio. One of the most predictable features of any criminal record office is the steady ringing of telephones and the movement of staff plying back and forth between the phones and the files.

In some cases the teleprinter or telex, found in every criminal record office, serves as substitute for the telephone. Every police force, and some individual police stations, possess a teleprinter which, although used much less frequently than the telephone, figures importantly when the message is urgent or when a written record of the exchange is required. Through the use of the teleprinter every police force in the country can be notified within as little as ten minutes of urgent matters like the flight of a dangerous criminal.

For other purposes, much information exchange takes place in writing. This is especially true with respect to communications of the detail of persons' criminal records, in connection with court appearances. There most communication takes place via the standard series of 'criminal record' forms discussed above. As the following discussion will show, forms are made out by the local police and passed back and forth at prescribed stages during the prosecution of accused persons. These forms, whose processing accounts for one of the major expeditures of resources by criminal record offices, do not pass through the mails, but travel daily back and forth between the local police and the criminal record office by police courier.

A third trunk line of communication in police surveillance is what are termed 'police informations'. These are the small bulletins circulated internally among the police. The largest and most widely circulated of these is the *Police Gazette*, published six times per week by New Scotland Yard, and distributed in quantity to every police force. It contains information on crimes and criminals throughout Britain, especially in those cases where action by police outside the area where the crime occurred is deemed necessary. Thus there are listings of stolen property, wanted and missing persons, and serious unsolved crimes, as well as routine cancellations of previous notices where crimes have been solved, property recovered, wanted or missing persons located, and so on.

... In the event of conviction, the scene is already set to enter the appropriate records in the individual's criminal record, or to create such a record if this is the first offence. The record of conviction, including the charge, the court, the date and the sentence, will be added to the descriptive form, and that form, along with the copy of the antecedents sheet, will go via the regional office to New Scotland Yard. Travelling the same route will be the individual's photos and fingerprints. The new data will be copied and entered in the appropriate regional files, as well as in the national repositories. The system does not work perfectly in this respect, and some convictions go unrecorded. But David Steer reports in his paper 'Recorded Convictions' that ninety-six per cent of 624 convictions in his sample did make their way to the Metropolitan Criminal Record Office, and the remaining four per cent were largely for relatively minor offences.

In the event of acquittal, the police generally destroy the data which they have developed in the course of their preparations. Some criminal record office spokesmen have gone to great lengths, in their conversations with me, to insist that no form of 'black mark' remains in their records as the result of acquittal. Other criminal record offices do retain certain information generated in prosecutions leading to acquittals, and practices vary considerably among the various offices. Some CROs, for example, retain photographs of acquitted persons, if such persons already possess criminal records whose photos are out of date. Elsewhere, information may be retained after acquittal if the charges have involved matters considered by the police especially serious or especially likely to be repeated —sexual offences being the prime example. And, of course, many criminal record offices do not hesitate to update their records whenever they can, so that current address and other information generated in the course of unsuccessful prosecutions will find its way into the criminal record file.

Finally, this entire system is likely to undergo considerable changes when the bulky paper files yield to the computerised information bank.

33C James B. Rule
COMPUTERISATION OF POLICE RECORDS

Since the 1960s preparations have been under way for the computerisation of police record-keeping. The essence of the plan is simple in its ambitiousness: to convert all records, regional and national, from criminal record offices and, ultimately, fingerprints offices, to computer storage in a single central location. The point of centralisation is to be the Police National Computer in London, which is to serve all police forces throughout Britain. To oversimplify only slightly, the announced aim of the system will be to provide the same qualitative services now provided by the national and regional record offices, but to do so much more quickly and efficiently from the single computerised centre.

Storage will be on discs, rather than tapes, so that the police can interrogate their files and update the information kept there immediately. Access is to be through terminals maintained in the headquarters of every police force in Britain, and, ultimately, in many local police stations as well. Plans provide for two kinds of terminals. One is to be a keyboard console, combined with a screen or visual display unit. Inquiries would be tapped into the central record with the keyboard, and responses would appear on the screen. The other terminal would resemble a telex machine, with inquiries typed in and responses typed out. One of the most important benefits of the system, according to the planners, will be the speed with which the machine can respond to queries; responses are predicted to be forthcoming to either terminal within ten seconds of submitting the request. Thus the constable on the beat or in his patrol car would radio a stop check request to his nearest terminal, and from there to the central file, and back again. The most optimistic predictions from the police envisage that the policeman making the request will be answered in less than half a minute.

As I have said, the long-term assumption has been that all criminal record files ultimately will be susceptible to computer storage. There are even plans for computerised storage of fingerprints, and for programming the machines to sort incoming prints against the entire collection. There are, however, considerable obstacles in the way of computerising the more discursive, voluminous files like the criminal records themselves. It is very difficult to say when the computerised storage of these materials in their full form will be operational. The final computerisation of fingerprint files will also require at least several years from the time of this writing. On the other hand, there are concrete and realistic plans for prompt computerisation of some of the simpler indices. The computer itself is being delivered at the time of this writing in 1971, and its initial experimental operations should begin in 1972. As one of the planners explained to me, the first goals will be to make operational the index of stolen vehicles; then the wanted and missing persons index, including the listing of disqualified drivers; and then the nominal index, the latter to enable the police to determine whether persons are 'known' to them. The computerisation of other indices is to follow once the first three have become successfully operational.

SOURCE: James B. Rule. *Private Lives and Public Surveillance* (1973)

WATCHDOGS OF LOYALTY

Almost every nation on earth has a police force additional to its regular and familiar police force. This 'secret police'—the term is unofficial but pretty accurate—is concerned with security against political threats. Britain has two such organisations, one semi-secret or at all events rather discreet regarding its activities, the other protected by deeper secrecy. The former is the Special Branch of the regular police, whose members are known to occupy themselves in observing demonstrations, taking the names of speakers at political meetings, and keeping an eye on the offices of extremist or minority movements. From time to time, there has been some concern about the activities of the Special Branch on the score of privacy. For instance, the Special Branch is allowed to tap telephones and open mail in rare cases with the express permission of the Home Secretary, but certain incidents have given rise to suspicion that it does so a good deal more often than it admits.

The other 'secret police' has the curious name of MI5. The Army traditionally lists its departments in this style—AG6, for example, is a branch of the Adjutant-General's Department—and MI5 means Military Intelligence 5. However, it is not a part of the armed forces any more than of the regular police, and it is not answerable to the Minister of Defence. It reports direct to the Prime Minister, and he alone (if he chooses, which is not often) answers questions about it from MPs. The staff, the budget, the address, and the name of the head of MI5 are not made public.

MI5 is concerned with security, in the sense of protecting the State against subversion and spying carried on in the interests of foreign nations. In the modern world, this task has heavy political and ideological connotations. The nations regarded as constituting a threat are primarily those of the communist bloc, to which Britain and her allies have been opposed throughout the period of the 'cold war'. But Britain also has a Communist Party, which enjoys a legal status and has a right to advocate the policies in which it believes, including friendship with the Soviet Union. And there are other organisations—Maoist, Trotskyist, anarchist—as radical as the CP, if not more so. In principle, members of all these groups are entitled to the same rights—including generally recognised rights to privacy—as other citizens.

A study of this situation, and of the activities of MI5, was made in 1956–7 by the Campaign for the Limitation of Secret Police Powers, which produced two pamphlets on the subject. The cases cited in these pamphlets were supplied mainly by MPs on the basis of information from constituents. I should perhaps apologise for quoting from such relatively dated documents; but MI5 seems to have become more circumspect in its methods, for MPs learned of no further cases and the Campaign was unable to pursue its activities. But the standards governing the work of MI5 are still in force and are undoubtedly applied.

What led to the formation of this Campaign was the appearance in 1956 of a White Paper which set these standards. Some notorious cases —especially that of Burgess and Maclean—had evoked an outcry about the laxness of British security. The Government appointed a committee of Privy Councillors to frame new and stricter security rules, and published a White Paper based on their report. It is worth noting that, while the White Paper was short, the report itself was long and most of it remains secret to this day. The White Paper said: 'It would not be in the public interest to publish the full text of the report or to make known all its recommendations.'

According to the White Paper: 'Whereas once the main task to be guarded against was espionage by foreign powers carried out by professional agents, today the chief risks are presented by communists and by other persons who for one reason or another are subject to communist influence.' It followed that such persons should not be employed on what was called 'secret work', and the White Paper added: 'An individual who is living with a wife or husband who is a communist or a communist sympathiser may, for that reason alone, have to be moved from secret secret work.' Liability to blackmail was another worry in the eyes of the Privy Councillors, and the document goes on to say: 'There is a duty on departments to inform themselves of serious failings such as drunkenness, addiction to drugs, homosexuality, or any loose living.'

The source of information, obviously, would in most cases be in the same office as the suspect. The White Paper put in a caution against 'tale-bearing or malicious gossip', but it laid down in the next sentence:

'It is important to impress not only on heads of departments but on supervisory officers generally that it is their duty to know their staff and that they must not fail to report anything which affects security.'

On this basis, suspects were sometimes transferred to non-secret work, sometimes dismissed altogether, and sometimes—as we shall see—disadvantaged in other ways. Often, neither the suspect himself, nor others who might have tried to defend him, found out what was alleged against him. The White Paper said: *'Decisions have sometimes to be taken without revealing full details of the supporting evidence.'*

And a minatory note was struck when the White Paper concluded: *'It is right to continue the practice of tilting the balance in favour of offering greater protection to the security of the State rather than in the direction of safeguarding the rights of the individual.'*

Analysing these doctrines, the Campaign for the Limitation of Secret Police Powers replied:

34A CLSPP
STATE SECURITY RISKS

The processes of British law are not suspended when spies are caught. They are tried exactly like murderers, burglars, or bigamists. They appear before judge and jury, are defended by counsel, can be convicted only on evidence heard in court, and are presumed innocent until found guilty. The only difference is that the press and public are excluded—and that not always. The aim of the State is to bring real spies to book and to avoid the error of supposing men to be spies who are not. In short, to find out about spying.

However, we now have the Government's word for it that the entire structure of individual rights can be set aside when a man is accused, not of actually spying, but of the crime of potentially spying. To become a unique pariah in modern Britain, it is sufficient to be the kind of man who, because of Communist sympathies or associations or of character defects, *might* spy or *might* be the involuntary tool of a spy. Such a man can be sacked without trial, by the arbitrary action of the executive branch of Government.

An argument to be met at this point is that dismissal from a job is not a punishment. Nobody is proposing to fine or imprison the 'security risk.' All that is being done is to protect the security of places of work that would be better off without his presence.

But the sack may be anything from a disaster to a relief. A civil servant, say, who has a medical degree or writes best-selling detective stories in his spare time can smile if he is dismissed on security grounds, especially if he is young. A man in late middle age who has spent his whole adult life in the Foreign Office or the electronics industry and is trained for nothing else sustains a shattering and irremediable blow if this happens to him. To say that he is not being punished is a cruel sophistry.

But, it is said, nobody has a right to work in the Foreign Office or in an electronic laboratory. A job is a privilege, granted at will by the employer and therefore to be withdrawn at will. We need to be very clear about where this argument leads. None of our rights, as has been said, date from time immemorial. All began as privileges. The right to worship was once a privilege of members of the Established Church. The right to vote was once a privilege of men of property.

A right, in fact, is simply a privilege so regularly granted and so broadly extended that it can be no longer denied by those in power. The position is admirably summed up by Dean Acheson, the US Secretary of State in the Truman administration, in his book, *An American Vista*:

'Freedom is preserved not by drawing distinctions between rights and privileges, but by our demanding and maintaining rights in privileges.'

Various facts enabled the writer of the CLSPP pamphlet to warn:

34B CLSPP
EMPLOYMENT RESTRICTIONS

The practice of limiting employment on security grounds is widening its radius. It began in the 'sensitive' Ministries (Service departments, Foreign Office, Ministry of Supply) and such Government establishments as Harwell. It now encompasses the whole civil service and many industrial firms making military equipment on contract. The manufacture of arms nowadays is so dispersed throughout the engineering industry that there is scarcely such a thing as 'the armaments industry.' A firm may be employing one workshop and a minority of employees on secret radar equipment while most of the business is devoted to ordinary wireless sets. But since the firm has only one personnel manager it is simpler to apply security conditions to the whole staff. Another firm, perhaps, is doing no defence work, but is seeking a defence contract; it tries to improve its standing by doing the same.

And what of employment that has no connection with defence at all? These things have already happened:

The Renfrewshire County Council refused to employ a qualified teacher, Mrs Stein, because her husband was a communist. The shortage of teachers is particularly acute in Scotland.

A young woman employed as a cashier at a club for civil servants at Cheltenham was dismissed because her husband belonged to the Young Communist League . . .

A technical assistant at the Armstrong Whitworth aircraft factory in Coventry, G. F. Clarke, was recently dismissed and told on inquiry that he was a Communist Party branch secretary. Mr. Clarke has been a member of the Labour Party for eight years. As it happens, there was a prominent Communist in Coventry with the not uncommon name of Clarke. The Minister of Supply covered this howler by refusing any inquiry and by saying that the initiative had been taken by the factory's management; they, however, told Clarke that they had acted on MI5 instructions. Those who imagine that injustice is always corrected should know that Clarke has not been reinstated.

An Austrian boy, who had come to Britain as a refugee, was living at Coventry at the age of sixteen. He and half a dozen other young Austrians spent regular social evenings together, and he collected a small sum from each to hire a room at the YMCA. Years later, having become a research engineer and a British subject, he found himself refused visas to the USA and Canada. Inquiries made by cousins in America disclosed that the black mark on his record was having been 'treasurer of the Young Austrians of Coventry.' But the British security services could not admit that their American counterparts had blundered. The rash young Austrian has since been accepted for two technical posts 'subject to clearance', and in the end rejected for both jobs.

. . . There was no proof that Mr. John Rex had been done out of a job by 'security'—until a Minister made a verbal slip. Mr. Rex is of South African origin. While he was at Rhodes University College, there was an argument over whether African students should be allowed to join the National Union of South African Students; Mr. Rex thought that they should.

After graduating with distinction he was offered a post in Southern Rhodesia. Six weeks after arriving there, he received notice that the Government considered him 'undesirable as an inhabitant or visitor, because of information received . . . from another Government'. His friends protested, but he had to go; the Minister of Justice declined to relent, complaining later that Rex had written a 'violent' letter to the *New Statesman*.

Mr. Rex returned to South Africa, and then got a job in this country as a staff tutor in Leeds University. While he was applying for a passport, a CID sergeant visited him and rather oddly showed him a letter marked **Most Secret**. In it he was described, in the picturesque jargon of apartheid-minded officialdom, as 'a believer in the teachings of Marx and Lenin and opposed to academic segregation'.

After three years at Leeds, he was asked by the Director of Extra-mural Studies at Durham University (who was concerning himself with finding staff for new colleges in Africa) to apply for a job at Fourah Bay College, Sierra Leone. He did—and was turned down. Later, Prof. Raybould, who was going to Ibadan College in Nigeria, asked Mr. Rex to apply for a job there, since the college was desperately short of extra-mural tutors. This appointment had only to go before the college senate for final approval, when the Principal asked for a delay 'as certain inquiries were pending'. Mr. Rex was turned down again.

Probably not even MI5 considers John Rex to be a Communist or a security risk. But, just as our secret police would expect the South African authorities to refuse admission to anyone on their books, so they reciprocate by victimising a man who has fallen foul of Strydom by opposing apartheid. And on this subject Mr. Rex holds strong views. He is secretary of the West Riding Council for African Affairs, whose president is that notorious subversive, Father Huddleston. He has written to the press to argue against Central African Federation. On these subjects his views might be highly popular in Sierra Leone and Nigeria—which may be why the South African authorities don't want him to go there.

All this was suspected by Labour MPs, and they said so in the House of Commons. The Colonial Secretary, Mr. Oliver Lyttelton, said that the cancellation of Mr. Rex's appointment to Fourah (the Ibadan episode came later) had nothing to do with his views on Federation.

Cancellation? Asked to explain the word, Mr. Lyttelton apologised for his mistake; the appointment had not been cancelled, he said next time the matter came up—it had never been decided on. It was an odd mistake, all things considered.

These young men, like anyone else, have to make their way in the world, and in competitive professions. When an employer scans a list of applicants for a job, he is an exceptional man if he makes further inquiries before crossing out the name beside which is noted: 'Refused entry to other Commonwealth countries on security grounds.' As great a handicap would be: 'Refused commission in Forces on security grounds.' But a number of young men will bear this tag all their lives.

John Clother has an honours degree in physics and his tutors have forecast a brilliant career for him. While doing his national service, he not only passed the officer selection board but also went through the entire cadet course and passed out with high marks. He had almost sewn his first pip on his uniform when a sympathetic commanding officer showed him a letter from the War Office: 'Sapper J. Clother, R.E., 23182346, is on no account to be commissioned.'

What has John Clother done? Nothing—but guilt in the eyes of MI5 is hereditary. Mr. Gordon Clother, John's father, who is a registrar and a justice of the peace at Gillingham, has long been active in the Labour Party and the Peace Pledge Union. Rightly or wrongly—and the War Office declines to state its side of the case—he thinks that his son has suffered for this.

So, apparently, has young A., who has asked us to withhold his name. His father is a doctor and a member of the Medical Association for the Prevention of War, regarded by officialdom as a Communist front, though its adherents protest that only two members of its executive are Communists, and Dr. A. certainly is not. He has in fact belonged to the Labour Party all his adult life; his son has never belonged to anything.

Young A., having passed the board for officer training in the Air Force, arrived at the training centre—and was sent straight back. He was told that orders to cancel his training had been received from the Air Ministry, but no reason was given.

Mr. Christopher Soames, Under-Secretary for Air, has provided an explanation. A., he writes, never passed the selection board; he was 'drafted in error' to the cadet unit. 'When this error was discovered his cadet training was cancelled.' Mr. Soames sent his regrets and added: 'It is our well-established practice not to disclose our reasons for regarding a candidate as unsuitable.'

. . . The Navy has proved itself no more gallant in these matters than the Army or the Air Force. Mr. A. E. Henderson passed a Commissions Board and was made a probationary midshipman; he then went, with thirty others, to study Russian at London University under a joint Services scheme. On the first day of the course the students were told that none of them would be removed unless after failing two examinations.

After the first examination, several of the students were told their marks; but when the results were published, they all found themselves ten marks lower than the original figure. Later the Admiralty's spokesman in Parliament, Commander Noble, explained that the civilian teachers had been marking too generously.

Henderson emerged with 49 marks, the pass mark being 50. He and two others were removed from the course; seven men, who had lower marks, were kept on. Those who left the course also lost their commissions, which was contrary to the normal rule.

Henderson concluded that he had been the victim of an injustice; but it was only much later, after the end of his national service, that he discovered that he was a security risk. He happened to meet the headmaster of his old preparatory school, who recounted that he had been visited twice by total strangers who asked him to 'confirm' that Henderson was a Communist. Then, at Oxford, Henderson was accepted into the University Air Squadron pending Air Ministry approval—which was not granted.

Henderson, who was in fact a Conservative, was completely mystified by his experiences. He wrote to his MP: 'Either I was maliciously accused of being a Communist, or I was suspected by some well-meaning idiot as a result of some remark (as anyone could be), or else I am carrying the can for someone else.'

One more case:

34C CLSPP
SECURITY CHECK

The firm that really twisted and turned, however, is that for which Miss Christina Shepherd worked as a draughtswoman. Why she is a security risk, nobody knows. She says of herself:

'I am not a Communist, a Communist sympathiser, a drunkard, or drug addict or any kind of sex pervert; I have never belonged to any political society. And as far as I know none of my friends or family are any of these things either. My parents and I have always voted Liberal if we bother to vote at all. I spend most of my spare time either gardening, cycling, dressmaking, or with my boy friends. I am quite prepared to have all my activities checked up and broadcast publicly.'

Miss Shepherd worked in London for a contract office, under a firm with headquarters in the Midlands. When it was announced that draughtsmen were needed for a spell with another firm, she volunteered, since she had worked there before and it was near her home. The same day, she was told that the work was secret, that there had been a security check, and that she alone had not passed it. 'I was also told,' she writes, 'that they had nothing against me personally or my work, and they would like me to remain in the London office.'

But this was not good enough for Miss Shepherd. She consulted her clergyman, who wrote to the managing director. He replied 'that it was a mistake to have informed me in the first place that I was a security risk and that if this upset me would I please accept their apologies.'

Miss Shepherd wrote to the Home Office, enclosing this letter. The Ministry of Supply, to whom the matter was passed, merely answered that the managing director's letter 'will have relieved your mind of any anxiety as to your employer's opinion of your integrity and reliability'. But she was still a security risk.

So Miss Shepherd wrote to her MP and to a newspaper. She

also saw her immediate boss and asked what were the charges against her and what was the source of the 'instruction' on which he said he was acting. He answered neither question, but told her that she was making things difficult for him. This was also the view of the managing director, who came to London, says Miss Shepherd, 'and told me that I was making a lot of trouble for the firm, and that although they did not want to sack me they could not tolerate trouble-makers'.

Miss Shepherd did not back down, and she was sacked. But so were all the female staff in the office. It abruptly became the policy of the firm not to employ draughtswomen.

SOURCE: Campaign for the Limitation of Secret Police Powers. *The Secret Police and You* (1956) and *A Year with the Secret Police* (1957)

PUBLIC SERVANTS AND PRIVATE PEOPLE

Millions of people, of course, go through life without any brushes with the police, secret or otherwise. In our complex society, however, it is virtually impossible to manage without repeatedly having dealings with officials of one kind and another. We file income tax returns, we contribute to National Insurance, we obtain licences for our cars and television sets; and we recognise that we can be penalised for evading these responsibilities, or for making false statements in connection with them.

The erosion of privacy has been gradual but inevitable. In a fine oratorical flight, the Earl of Chatham declared in 1763: 'The poorest man may in his cottage bid defiance to all the force of the Crown. It may be frail; its roof may shake; the wind may blow through it; the storms may enter; the rain may enter—but the King of England cannot enter; all his forces dare not cross the threshold of the ruined tenement.' Today, about 10,000 officials and inspectors enjoy a statutory right to enter private premises in Britain.

Just as the police cannot do their work without information about actual or suspected criminals, so officials in central and local government —officials concerned with housing, education, and the ramifications of welfare services—cannot do their work without information about the

H

*rest of us. While conceding this, we do well to be on our guard against
the tendency of some officials to gather information for its own sake, or
without adequate justification, and to intrude on privacy in the process.*

Here is an example:

35A NCCL
INFORMATION OBTAINED FROM
OFFICIAL SURVEYS

In September 1968 the Department of Employment and
Productivity carried out an earnings survey, based on a sample
of employees. When, early in 1970, a second survey was carried
out, some persons and organisations became alerted to the
inherent danger to privacy, and voices in protest were heard
from varied quarters.

The survey took a random sample of employees (based on
N.I. numbers) and required employers, under the Statistics of
Trade Act 1947, to furnish a great deal of very personal information about them. The survey was on one in 100 workers
throughout the country, and the questions to be answered
included the nature of employees' work, details of wages,
information about attendance, whether this is regular, whether
he is a late arrival or early finisher, whether he has changed his
job and how often, whether he has been directly or indirectly
involved in any industrial dispute, whether he has any history
of uncertificated illness, and so on.

The issue was ventilated in the press, and the NCCL had
complaints from such widely varying sources as a Rural District
Council, the Director of a manufacturing company and someone in the personnel department of an insurance company.

These were not people complaining about the invasion of
their own privacy, but responsible employers drawing attention
to the dangers on behalf of their staff, whom the Act did not
even require to be consulted.

Another example, this time in the sphere of local government:

35B NCCL
STAINES HOUSING DEPARTMENT'S FILES

Upon visiting the Housing Department at Staines, Middlesex, a Mrs Maureen Cooke discovered to her distress her file which contained a newspaper report of a court case in which she had been involved four years earlier . . . That the Cooke case was only the tip of the iceberg was suggested by the remark of a spokesman for the GLC that 'every local authority has files on its tenants' . . . The item on Mrs Cooke related to something that had happened when she was only seventeen and before her marriage. Further, Mr Hemsley (a Councillor) disclosed that officials had refused to confirm or deny that files were available to other Council departments. His suggestion that tenants and applicants should be allowed to see their files was refused . . .

The fear that the Staines practice might be repeated else-where was confirmed when Gloucester's council later admitted that it keeps newspaper reports of court cases involving its tenants. At the same time, Hereford's city council was accused by one of its members of following the same practice.

Following the revelations, the NCCL appealed to the then Minister of Housing and Local Government, Mr. Peter Walker, to take action in the form of a general circular to councils, with recommendations on the issue.

The Minister declined to intervene, on the grounds that 'on the strength of two or three local Press reports I would not be justified in issuing a circular reminding them of the respon-sibility of which they are, I believe, already aware'.

SOURCE: National Council for Civil Liberties evidence to the Younger Committee

Officials who hold a particularly powerful position are those of the Supplementary Benefits Commission. It arises from the duality of the

British welfare system: firstly there are National Insurance benefits—unemployment, sickness, and retirement pensions—of fixed amounts to which those concerned are entitled by virtue of having paid contributions; and secondly, for anyone still left below the poverty line, there are supplementary benefits of variable amounts paid at the discretion of Social Security officials. These officials, who are not professionally trained and are rather badly paid themselves, are continually involved in making delicate decisions, for the number of claimants to SB has risen steadily for a generation and is well over the 2 million mark. Among them are thousands of women under the age of sixty (after sixty they would get a retirement pension) who are unable to work, or anyway to earn an adequate income, because they have dependent children, and have no male breadwinner in the household because they are widowed, divorced, separated or unmarried. In 1971 there were 278,000 such women on the SB books.

If a woman in this position is found to be living with a man—in official jargon, cohabiting—who thus assumes an obligation to provide for her, her benefit can be reduced or withdrawn. To decide whether cohabitation exists, the Commission resorts to questioning and if necessary to investigation. There were sixteen investigators in 1954 and 326 in 1972. Figures for 1971 show that 10,521 claimants were investigated on suspicion either of cohabitation or of falsely claiming to be deserted, of whom 4,712 had their allowances reduced or withdrawn and some were moreover prosecuted for fraud. In certain cases, women found to be cohabiting also lost their widows' pensions (a National Insurance benefit). The Exchequer was saved £887,000, or rather £487,000 after allowing for the costs of investigation.

Women thus affected can appeal to a tribunal, but it is clear that many do not know of their rights or choose not to appeal from fear of publicity.

An official statement tells us:

36 DHSS
COHABITATION

The question at issue is whether or not an unmarried couple are living together as man and wife or, in the language of the

Act, cohabiting. In most cases, where the couple wish to be regarded as married, there is no difficulty. What is not always understood is that, even if a couple do not regard themselves as husband and wife, the Commission has a duty to decide whether, for the purposes of entitlement to supplementary benefit, they must be treated as if they were.

The Act does not define cohabitation. What the Commission has to decide is whether the relationship between the man and the woman is such that they must be regarded as living as man and wife in the ordinary sense of the term. There is no simple way of deciding the issue. The existence of a sexual relationship is not in itself decisive and certainly occasional sleeping together does not constitute cohabitation. The fact that a man is contributing to a woman's financial support does not necessarily mean that she is cohabiting with him. On the other hand, if he does not support her financially that is not in itself conclusive evidence against cohabitation.

The main criteria taken into account are

> Does the woman use the man's name and do they represent themselves, or are they publicly acknowledged, as man and wife?
>
> Is the partnership a stable one? How long has it lasted?
>
> Is there a common home, in the sense of shared accommodation and household duties?
>
> Have the couple had children? Do they share the same bedroom?

... Instructions to the Commission's staff emphasise that the cohabitation rule is not based on moral grounds and that a decision must be strictly in accordance with the facts of the particular case.

SOURCE: Department of Health and Social Security. *Supplementary Benefits Handbook* (1972)

But this is not the whole story, according to Ruth Lister, Legal Research

*Officer of the Child Poverty Action Group, who has made a study of the
situation based on information from fifty women investigated for alleged
cohabitation. She points out that the* vade mecum *for officials is not
the published Handbook but the instructions given to officials and contained in the 'A' and 'AX' codes. These are not available to claimants
or to the public and Miss Lister gained access to them only unofficially.
In the 'AX' code particularly, she comments, 'the general emphasis on
impartiality presented in the Report (ie the Supplementary Benefits
Commission's 1971 Report on this question) gives way to one on proving
guilt'. The code states, for example: 'The aim of the observation is to
provide evidence of the man's movements that lead to the conclusion that
he lives in the claimant's accommodation.' Miss Lister continues:*

37A Ruth Lister
COHABITATION AND THE 'AX' CODE

The approach taken in the 'AX' code is very different. There
is no question of following the official 'combination of facts'
approach and of carefully weighing up all the facts of the situation. Indeed the whole question of establishing whether cohabitation exists or not is virtually ignored. Instead, all the
criteria carefully elaborated by the Commission are collapsed
into the one overriding criterion of whether there is a man living
in the same accommodation as the woman. There is no mention
of the stipulation made by the Supplementary Benefits Commission in their official report, of the necessity of establishing
that they are living together as man and wife. The important
issue of housekeeping and financial arrangements is summarily
dismissed with the instruction 'that the financial arrangements
the couple come to in their relationship is not the point at issue.
They may, however, be of interest in that, if there has been
regular maintenance, the evidence of cohabitation will have
been even further strengthened.'

What is even more disturbing is that one of the instructions
implies that proof of actual cohabitation is not necessarily of

primary importance in deciding whether to withdraw a woman's benefit. As an example of the difficulties of getting acceptable evidence for bringing a prosecution, it states, 'the birth of a child would indicate there has been at least a temporary liaison but it may not be held to be proof of a regular cohabitation. It may, nevertheless, be sufficient reason for regarding the woman as looking to the man for maintenance'. This casts serious doubts on the assertion in the Handbook quoted above that 'the decision depends solely on whether it appears that the couple are living as man and wife in the full sense of the term, not on any moral consideration or on whether the man and woman have slept together on occasions'.

The instructions to officers contained in the 'AX' code as to how to proceed in cases of suspected cohabitation are considerably more detailed than those contained in the 'A' code. For this reason and for those outlined above, it is not totally unjustified to suggest that it is the 'AX' code which provides the main framework in which investigations into suspected cohabitation are carried out and that as a result the list of criteria of cohabitation carefully drawn up by the Supplementary Benefits Commission are not uppermost in officers' minds. This, together with the fact that, as the Supplementary Benefits Commission itself admits in its Report, 'the decision on whether or not cohabitation exists is, in the last resort, a matter of personal judgement' and officers, like the rest of the community, have their values and prejudices, goes a long way to explain the number of cases where the cohabitation rule has been wrongly applied.

From knowledge of actual cases, Miss Lister writes:

37B Ruth Lister
INDIVIDUAL CASES INVESTIGATED

In seven cases, it was clear from the responses that the couple were not simply living in the same house but were living *to-*

gether, eating at the same table and sleeping in the same bed. In six of these cases the woman was prosecuted for fraud. However, although at first sight these may appear as clear cut cases of cohabitation, they do highlight some of the problems involved in operating the rule. Although the men were mostly willing to contribute to their own, and their own children's, keep and some were also willing to contribute to the woman's, they did not feel responsible for any other children the woman might have. As one man earning a very low wage put it: 'I'm a single man, why should I be made to keep another man's kids?'

As well as being vulnerable financially, many of the women had relationships that were not themselves particularly secure and in three cases it is known that the men subsequently left them. In one case, not prosecuted for fraud, the woman readily admitted the existence of a common-law marriage but the problem lay in the currently sporadic nature of the man's presence, as the relationship was in its last stages before breaking down completely.

A woman claiming benefit who takes in a male lodger runs the risk of being told to look to the man for her support, particulary if there is the least bit of evidence of friendly relations between the two. This happened to a widow, Mrs. Jones, whose case was taken up by the Citizens' Rights Office after she had been deprived of both her widow's mothers allowance and her supplementary benefit. The DHSS had acted originally on information from 'a member of the public' that Mrs. Jones and her lodger were living together. Mrs. Jones was represented at the National Insurance tribunal by the CRO. The case presented by the Insurance Officer was that the relationship was more than that of a landlady and lodger because the two were friendly and she said that she liked him. Also he sometimes helped keep the children in order and occasionally bought them some clothes. Mrs. Jones' representative argued that none of the evidence presented was inconsistent with a normal relationship between landlady and lodger and asked whether it is necessary for a landlady to prove that she *disliked* her male lodger to escape an accusation of cohabitation. The tribunal dismissed the Insurance Officer's case as being unsubstantiated.

A slightly different situation was that of Mrs. White. She had met the father of her youngest child back in 1970 and had moved into a room on the top floor of his mother's house. He had never lived with her but had slept with her at times, though not since the beginning of 1971. He had at least one other woman by whom he had also had a child and, as far as Mrs. White knew, he rarely stayed at his mother's house though he used it as an accommodation address. He paid her £2 a week maintenance for the baby and came to visit her about twice a week when he would see the baby, chat and watch the television. Mrs. White appealed to a tribunal but lost.

. . . In a couple of cases where the woman was prosecuted for fraud the man had been staying to help her out for a particular reason. In one case it was the woman's boyfriend whom she had asked to stay with her to protect her against her husband who had been threatening and pestering her since she had started divorce proceedings against him. Her boyfriend was supporting neither her nor her three children and had always told her that he refused to do so but would give her a bit of money to cover any meals she cooked for him. The other woman, a divorcee, had had a major operation and had been told by the doctor to take it easy and not to lift things for six months. A friend came to stay with her to help her look after the children. He left when her benefit was withdrawn as, having to pay maintenance to his own family, he had no intention of supporting her.

The most common situation of all was that where the woman had a boyfriend who visited her and sometimes stayed the night, but who gave her no financial support, and who certainly did not consider himself to be living with her as her husband. This again suggests that undue attention is paid by officers to the question of sexual relations.

A typical case was that of Mrs. Brown. Her boyfriend had been a friend of her husband's from whom she was separated.

He had continued seeing her after the separation out of sym-
pathy and had started staying the night. He usually slept at
Mrs. Brown's four or five times a week, but considered his
home to be at his mother's. He kept all his clothes in his bed-
room at his mother's house and contributed to her household
expenses. He went home each morning to collect his sand-
wiches and ate his evening meal with his mother. He made no
contribution to Mrs. Brown's household other than to provide
the Sunday lunch which he ate with them. He had no intention
of supporting Mrs. Brown and the question of marriage had
never been discussed. Mrs. Brown tried to make clear to the
officer that it was purely a sexual relationship, that 'Mr. X does
not live here, he just shares my bed'. However, neither the
Commission nor the appeal tribunal were able to grasp the
distinction that she made between a man staying with her and
his living with her. Similar examples are those of one alleged
cohabitee who was still living with his own wife, visiting the
claimant when he could, and of another, who lived with his
his mother and who, when he had stayed the night, would
return home to wash and shave.

Another case involved a widow who was in receipt of a
widowed mother's allowance and supplementary benefit for
herself and her daughter. Mrs. Green met the man about a year
after her husband's death and he began to visit her regularly in
the evenings, though only eating there irregularly. He lived
over a cafe and never spent the night at Mrs. Green's. After
about a year they were considering marriage but Mrs. Green
was worried about her daughter's reactions and therefore it was
decided that for a trial period he should just stay at weekends
(for two nights at a time because they thought this could not
jeopardise her benefit). The Monday following the first weekend
that he stayed, Mrs. Green went to the local DHSS office to tell
them of the arrangement they had agreed on. The DHSS re-
warded her honesty by taking away her order books the following day . . .

Miss Black was also prosecuted for fraud. She had lived with the father of one of her children back in 1963–64 but had not seen him since, until last year a friend of hers bumped into him. He was doing casual work and was living in a shed. He asked after Miss Black and went to see her. He visited her again on the child's birthday and then turned up one evening and asked her if she would wash a shirt for him. This she did and he started leaving one or two shirts with her regularly. He only stayed the night a couple of times, after they had been drinking. He gave her no money but occasionally gave her some fruit or vegetables off his stall in the market and she never cooked for him. The fact that she had taken the flat calling herself by his name was used as evidence against her, though her explanation of this, that she was afraid the landlord would not let to an unmarried mother, would appear to be perfectly reasonable.

The question of privacy arises most sharply in connection with the methods of investigation:

37C Ruth Lister
INVESTIGATORS AT WORK

In order to assess how discreet the investigators were in their observations, the women were asked if they were ever aware of investigators watching them. Of the 43, only seven had been aware of the investigators, usually having seen them parked outside their houses early in the morning. Thus, on the whole, the investigators appear to have been fairly unobtrusive in their observations. However, the experiences of some other women (not included in the study) that have come to our attention indicate that in a few instances the officers have been somewhat over-zealous in the exercise of their duties. For example, one woman in a small country town was trailed down the street by an investigator in a car. Several others were observed through their windows from a local authority flat opposite. In two other cases investigators were discovered kneeling and peering through the claimants' letter-boxes. (One of them, when asked what he was doing, replied that he was collecting the census form!)

Even though most of the women had not been aware of the investigators watching them, the discovery when presented with the investigators' evidence, that they had been doing so was rather unsettling. One young unsupported mother is now convinced that she is still being watched and is afraid that she will become paranoid about it.

The respondents were asked if they were visited at home by an investigator in order to discover how many allegations were backed up by personal visits. Although the great majority were visited (some even two or three times), it is disturbing to find that in five cases benefit was withdrawn without a visit having been made by an investigator. On the other hand, it is possible that these women were visited by an investigator without realising it . . .

The thoroughness with which the visits were conducted appears to have varied considerably. One woman told the investigator to look round the house so that he could see for himself that there was no evidence of a man's presence but the investigator refused. In other instances the investigators appear to have virtually forced their way in on the claimant. Despite the Commission's assurance that investigators 'are well aware that they have no right of entry into private premises except by invitation of the occupier', one woman wrote that two officers arrived early in the morning and that 'when I pointed out to one of them that he had no right to search, he said: "Oh yes I do, I have every right." ' Another woman was in bed, not feeling well, when the investigators made their visit, yet they still came in.

. . . The 11 women who said that their alleged cohabitee had been interviewed were asked whether the officer told them of this when they themselves were interviewed and, if so, whether they told them what the man had said. Of the nine women who replied, seven said that the investigator had told them of the interview but only three had been told what the man had said. One of these three, though, said that the man told her afterwards that he had not made the statement attributed to him by the officer. One man tried to make an appointment with the local DHSS office but they refused to see him on the grounds that it had nothing to do with him despite the fact that the woman was being told to look to him for support for herself and her children. Another man, who was interviewed, was so angry with the investigator's conduct that he made a written complaint to the Regional Controller. He was interviewed by two investigators at work. They did not give their names but said it was a matter of great importance. They asked him a number of intimate and embarrassing questions and one of them said: 'Tell us the truth and we'll let you off the hook—think carefully before you answer because your whole future depends on it'. When he refused to answer any more questions, the other one said, 'Since he refuses to answer, let's go to our legal department and get a summons, for I think he's guilty'. They also implied that it was a criminal offence to associate socially with the woman in question. The man felt that they had embarrassed him unnecessarily at his place of work.

. . . Those who received visits were asked whether the officer was civil to them. Only 13 of the 36 for whom information was available gave a positive answer and a further four gave qualified responses. The majority of them expressed some dissatisfaction with the officer's treatment of them and only one woman actually praised the officer for his helpfulness and understanding. This question aimed specifically at assessing the officers' attitudes and behaviour, but the responses, of course, represent the claimants' own subjective views of this. To a certain extent this is perfectly valid since it is the claimants' experiences in which we are interested. However, it is probably fair to say in some cases, as the Commission does, that the very fact of investigation may cause resentment which would colour the claimants' responses to this question. Nevertheless, the examples given of some of the officers' remarks suggests that the general negative response to the question is more than just a reflection of such a resentment.

The most common adjectives used to describe the officers' manner were 'arrogant', 'uncivil' and 'insulting'. A number of them complained that they were called a liar or that the officer implied that they were lying, and one that 'when he came he was very nasty and talked to me like a dog'.

Two of the women were particularly upset and embarrassed because the officer made his remarks in front of a third person. One of them was told in front of her daughter that 'Mr. X must either marry you or leave you'. The other woman who was prosecuted for fraud wrote: 'After the court case I was walking down the road just outside the court. I stood talking to a friend when the same officer and investigator who came to see me came across the road straight up to me and said smiling, "I'm glad you didn't get off lightly," and that I'd think twice before I did it again. I felt so ashamed as my friend hadn't a clue where I had been.'

The responses again showed an undue interest on the officers' part in the women's personal relationships which was resented by the women concerned. 'He talked as if I was dirty' was one of the complaints. One woman was interrogated at length about her relationships: did she earn money 'downtown', did she have men visitors, when did they leave, did they come back or did fresh ones come? Another was asked repeatedly whether she was sleeping with the alleged cohabitee. One officer even falsely accused a woman who was in hospital of being pregnant.

Further facts emerge from hearings at tribunals in cases when claimants were assisted by staff of the Child Poverty Action Group:

37D Ruth Lister
TRIBUNAL HEARINGS OF COHABITATION CASES

In supplementary benefit tribunals, the procedure normally followed by CPAG representatives is to argue their case using the Commission's own published criteria of cohabitation though these are not actually binding on the tribunal. A good example of where this was successful and, what is more, where it was clear from their written reasons for the decision that the tribunal had made their decision according to these criteria is provided by the case of a divorcee, Mrs. Peters, accused of cohabiting with her boyfriend. She was represented by CPAG's Citizens' Rights Office. The relationship between the couple was in their own eyes a casual one. The man stayed with her irregularly though never more than three or four times a week, and she did some of his washing and ironing. His only financial contribution was £5 a week to cover use of her telephone and the food that he ate there. The Commission's allegations were based on an anonymous phone call and on a special investigator's report that the man had been seen leaving the house four consecutive mornings. The presenting officer also claimed, at one stage, that all that is necessary to prove cohabitation is a common address and for a couple to sleep together. Using the *Supplementary Benefits Handbook* and the Commission's report on *Cohabitation*, Mrs. Peters' representative was able to argue that this is not in fact so and that, in this particular case, cohabitation, as 'defined' by the Commission's own criteria, had not been established. The tribunal accepted the argument and the appeal was allowed, though in reassessing her benefit, the Commission were instructed to take into account the £5 paid her weekly by the man. The reasons given by the tribunal for its decision were as follows: that there was no common home, no responsibility on the man's part for her children and no significant contribution made by him to the cost of maintaining her household.

The case also provided an example of how an experienced representative can challenge what at first sight appears as damaging evidence. Part of the presenting officer's case was that both the man and Mrs. Peters had, when questioned by the investigator, admitted to living as man and wife. In fact it came out at the hearing that she had thought the investigator was asking, euphemistically, if she were sleeping with the man, and when her representative asked the investigator to read out the actual notes that he had made, it became clear that the man had made no such admission.

. . . Apart from the fact that the alleged cohabitee, Mr. Z, was the father of one of Mrs. Brett's children, which was not in dispute, each piece of evidence presented by the Commission was effectively challenged. Explanations were given to the tribunal for two pieces of circumstantial evidence. Evidence quoted by the presenting officer from an education welfare officer and from neighbours that Mr. Z was living with Mrs. Brett was rejected by her representative as being merely hearsay and a neighbour was actually presented to the tribunal as witness that Mr. Z no longer lived with Mrs. Brett and had not been there since the weekend that Mrs. Brett claimed that he was last there (to see his son).

The presenting officer then called upon one of the two investigators present to make his report of his observations of Mrs. Brett's house. The investigator had watched the house on 14 occasions. He claimed to have seen Mr. Z twice with a dog which he knew to be Mrs. Brett's and on two other occasions had seen him in the area, that was all. When asked by her representative to give a description of Mr. Z he said he was five foot eight to nine inches tall, was broad to plump and sometimes wore glasses. As the neighbour, called as witness, later testified, he was, in fact, five foot two inches tall and never wore glasses. The investigator had not approached Mr. Z in order to identify him because, he said, he knew it was Mr. Z, having known him for some years. During the cross-examination, it came out that not only did Mrs. Brett have a neighbour of similar build to Mr. Z but also that this neighbour had an identical alsatian to Mrs. Brett's and that he sometimes visited her with the dog.

The presenting officer tried to dismiss the issue of inadequate identification as 'a matter of inches', not to be worried about. However, he was forced to admit that the evidence from the investigator's report was 'not conclusive'. 'It does not prove anything.' This, despite the fact that he had opened his case by saying that the Commission would never bring a case unless it was sure of its facts.

Mrs. Brett won her appeal and her benefit was restored. The question remains though, on this and all the other successful appeals, whether the outcome of the appeal would have been the same had she not been represented.

SOURCE: Ruth Lister. *As Man and Wife?* (Child Poverty Action Group, 1973)

PART THREE

Exposed Positions

THE MASS MEDIA

Many people, when they think of intrusion into privacy, are thinking primarily of the mass media—that convenient inclusive phrase for press, radio and television. It is the press that comes in for most of the criticism, partly because it is in private hands and unashamedly conducted for profit, partly because charges of triviality and sensationalism are easily made, and partly because journalists themselves are aware (as they have shown, for instance, at their trade union conferences) of the dubious methods sometimes used in news-gathering. An article which I wrote some years ago gives a short guide:

38 Mervyn Jones
REPORTERS AND THE PUBLIC

An analogy can usefully be made with the laws of war, which are beginning to look a bit silly in the nuclear age but which have governed fairly effectively for a couple of centuries. You don't, for example, shoot prisoners; you don't poison wells; you don't shell open towns. Obviously, these laws would be a mockery if the proviso were added to each of them: 'unless it is the only way to gain an advantage'. Such is the moral confusion that covers the world of journalism, that this proviso is implicitly tacked on to all the rules which are 'in theory' admitted. One often hears a reporter say, in defence of some conduct that he knows to be vile: 'It was the only way to get the story.' But what began, perhaps, as an extreme resort in the event of difficulty has long ago become a regular practice, at least with regard to certain types of story—those concerned with private lives. The reporter knows in advance that a straight inquiry will meet with a rebuff. He is bound, 'to get the story', to embark on the deliberate use of unethical methods. Nor should we pin the blame on him; editor and proprietor, in demanding this kind of story, know that they are enforcing this kind of method. It is clear that, if rules of journalistic method are to have force or meaning, they must be applied whatever the circumstances and whatever the cost. They must, if necessary, involve losing the story—or even not trying for the story in the first place.

Here are some of the methods I have in mind. Anyone in Fleet Street knows, even if the Press Council doesn't, that they are in repeated, if not in all instances systematic, use.

Simple Intrusion. When a person is the quarry of the press, he must reckon that reporters and photographers will use any method that is physically possible to get into his house. If he has a garden, they will climb over the wall. If it is summer, and a garden door or a window is open, they will come through it. If, hearing a ring, he opens the front door, they will march in *before* they start talking; few people remember to keep the door on a chain.

The householder is, supposedly, protected by the law of trespass, and in fact this has once or twice been successfully invoked against the press. Anybody entering another person's house without permission is a trespasser. However, unless the householder has suffered some real damage, a civil action for trespass can be a lengthy and unrewarding exercise. In any case, even if the gentlemen of the press can be induced or forced to leave within a short time, it may well be that they have already achieved their aim. This, quite often, is not to ask questions, but to get a photograph or to assure themselves of the presence of (say) another man's wife, or a child whose custody is disputed.

Pursuit. Next to having reporters in your house, there is nothing more intimidating than to look out of the window and see a posse of them at the wheels of their cars, ready to start up as soon as you emerge. To drive along with a couple of them ahead (keeping to the crown of the road lest you should overtake) and the rest following behind is an effective stop on freedom of movement. Neither in practical nor in moral terms is there any real difference between intrusion and pursuit. If I am already in X's house when the reporters push their way in, or if the reporters follow me to X's house and wait until I come out, the story is the same.

Deception. This is the customary means of intrusion, when physical force will not suffice; it is chiefly employed when the door is opened by someone other than the principal quarry— by a member of his family, a visitor, or a servant. The corniest device is to pretend to be the man who reads the meter. This is of use, principally, to the quick-fire photographer, since it will not get the intruder very far, except in. The reporter, mustering more ingenuity, will sometimes claim to be the friend of a friend and the bearer of a message; the reaction to this invented message will normally tell him what he wants to know. Other stratagems are suited to particular circumstances. Examples abound, and are jovially recounted in Fleet Street pubs. Here are three of recent date:

A mother, the day after giving birth to a baby, found her hospital room invaded by a young woman she'd never seen before. Equipped with a bunch of flowers, this reporter had represented herself to the staff as a relative. She stayed only long enough to read the cards on the other flowers, and they made the story.

A woman whose marriage was on the rocks was told by the caretaker at her block of flats that he had been questioned by private detectives paid by her husband. She knew that this procedure would be both untypical of her husband and, since she was giving him grounds for divorce, pointless. The 'detectives', of course, were reporters.

In my third and most nauseating example, it was thought desirable to prove that a successful business man was behaving meanly to his parents. They were questioned about how much money their son sent them by reporters posing as National Assistance Board officials.

. . . **Bad Faith.** This can take an infinity of forms, but it may be broadly defined as securing information for one (false) purpose and using it for another. Asked for a fact relating to my personal life, or to that of a friend, I might well refuse to supply it as the staple of a news story, but come out with it as a detail for a 'profile'. Many of the distinguished and the innocent have been caught this way; the profile never appears, but the news story or gossip paragraph does.

Lack of Respect for Confidences. 'Off the record' is an established convention, familiar to anyone who has to do with the press. True, it is often misused, especially by officials and politicians who tell a journalist something 'off the record' which he was likely to discover anyhow and which he now cannot publish. But, when properly used, it has this definite and useful meaning: 'You have a scrap of information which misleads unless explained; to instruct you in its significance, or lack of significance, I must tell you other private facts.'

. . . Of course, the victim is in a hopeless position from the start if he doesn't know that he is talking to the press. This may occur through a deception of the kind I have described. It may also occur because he is really not talking to a journalist, but to an informer—a man with an *entrée* in high society, politics, or some other private world, who regularly or occasionally sells information to the papers. Some of these people claim to be freelance journalists; others have ordinary jobs, disclaim and indeed conceal any connection with Fleet Street, and are simply spies. But the editor knows all about them, and more or less relies on them.

Threats. In theory, just as a reporter has a right to ask questions, anyone has a right to refuse to answer. However, this right is only a reality if the reporter then goes away. What he does, if he has been instructed that the story matters, is to say: 'I'm going to be here all today and another man's taking over tonight, and we'll go on asking until you decide to talk to us.' This is, in plain terms, a threat of persecution.

Another threat takes this form: 'Well, if you won't tell us, we know who to ask.' When you hear this, you know that the threat of persecution is being made against someone whose welfare is important to you—the friend you are shielding, the man or woman you love, or a child. Some of those stories about children being questioned on their way home from school are true. They don't occur often, because children are prone to give a garbled account of adult happenings which they don't understand, so this journalistic technique is rather a last resort; cases, however, are on record.

SOURCE: Mervyn Jones in *The Twentieth Century* (Spring 1962)

How do people feel when they have no privacy at all? A striking side-light on this question came from an interview which Brigitte Bardot gave at the height of her fame. Asked whether she read what was written about her, she replied:

39A 'The Twentieth Century'
INTERVIEW WITH BRIGITTE BARDOT

'IF BY chance I do read some of it, I become demoralised. It is always the same. None of it is *true*.'

What is true, then?

'I don't know myself. I don't know what the truth about me is. But I do know, when I read these things, what the lies are.'

We fell silent. Then I launched out into an odd speech. I explained that—whether one was called Stalin, Napoleon, de Gaulle or Bardot—it was almost the same thing from a certain point of view. You climb, step by step, to the heights of fame.

As you rise, the air becomes rarified, the vision gets blurred, you feel giddy, and when you are there, on top of the pyramid, you are alone. Isn't this true?

'Oh yes, that's the terrible thing. Yes, indeed. . . . I have perhaps four or five friends in all. My true friends are the ones I had when I was a girl.'

She longs to be a member of the ordinary crowd. But, like a pack of hounds, they devour her, tear her to pieces or—sell her. The hounds are ready to pounce.

'The slightest response on my part is worth ten or twenty thousand francs. Whatever move I make in life—it is saleable. This is terrible, you know.'

She was to tell me that solitude can go even further. That she feels like a prisoner. That she cannot go to the cinema or to the theatre. That she cannot go for a walk in the street. But what about her friends?

'People who talk to me don't behave naturally. I join a group, and there it is; people are no longer the same. This is dreadful. It's like being in a fairy-tale or rather a nightmare. And, at times, I feel I am not myself, either. And if I *am* myself and follow my impulses, that only gets me into trouble.

'I have been given everything, but I cannot make use of the gifts. And time is passing. I tell myself that time is passing and that I am fettered, a prisoner behind my own face. . . . I have always been very shy and this hasn't changed. It has become worse. If somebody recognises me I am disconcerted. I dread being recognised.'

Later, the interviewer asked whether she was putting up a pretence by speaking in this vein. Brigitte Bardot answered:

39B 'The Twentieth Century'
THE PUBLIC IMAGE

'No, not at all . . . If only you knew how much of a sham I feel . . . There are days when I feel absolutely rotten, and I find myself cheap and showy all the time. That's why I don't go out. People imagine they are going to see the seventh wonder of the world; but if I don't put on a mink and a hat, you should hear what they say. It depresses me. And as I have no confidence in myself anyway . . . What did give me confidence were the two appearances I made on TV. The first, because I could be myself and I had pals around me; the other, because I defended a cause which is close to my heart—the prevention of cruelty to animals.'

And what does she think of fame, her fame?

'If I were only what they say I am, empty-headed, with a bird's brain, and all that—I should be a nobody.'

What is the source of your fame then?

'By now it keeps going on its own impetus.'

SOURCE: *The Twentieth Century* (Spring 1962); translation of an interview first published in *L'Express*

The Younger Report surveyed the reasons for concern:

40A Younger Report
NEWSPAPER PUBLICITY

Two instances have been put to us of intrusion where no celebrity was concerned and there was no special urgency or importance involved in the news item. In the first, reporters pestered the occupants of a private house to obtain material for an article about witchcraft. In the second, a reporter called on parents late at night in their remote holiday house, at the end of a day in which police had been making a full-scale local search for a man who had attacked their daughter in the neighbourhood the previous day. However, a total of only four complaints to us by individuals of press intrusion, even if they reflect a small part of the total grievance, scarcely provide support for the view that unreasonable press intrusion is either common or growing.

The principal organisations to complain to us about press

activities were those with a professional or administrative responsibility for the welfare of others. Some organisations in the teaching profession, for instance, objected to press intrusion into school affairs and demanded greater care by reporters in seeking and conducting interviews, particularly with pupils and parents. The argument runs that schools are special communities, where the care of the pupils is assigned to the teachers by the normal guardians—the parents; schools have to be run on rules that do not apply outside; so if the press approach pupils direct, inside or outside the school, or even parents, or comment on the administration and discipline of a school without contacting the head, the results are a breach of the privacy of a partly closed community which is entitled to some of the same privacy as the home, and consequent damage to the delicate balance of discipline essential in schools.

A similar view, for a different reason, is advanced by some of the organisations in the medical profession, who criticise the press' disregard at times for the well-being of patients in hospital in their desire to get newsworthy stories or pictures. These organisations claim that proper care of patients requires that the work of hospitals and other medical institutions should be reasonably free from outside interference or disturbance.

The nub of many complaints against newspaper publicity is the identification of private persons involved in news stories. It may be that people prominent in public life also object to publication of their private activities, but we have received no complaints of this; it is however an important issue to have in mind in considering the problem of the right balance between privacy and the public interest. The complaints we have received—from people not in public life—all concern the coupling of identities with news publicity. The news concerned accidents, organ transplants, proceedings for minor criminal offences in the lower courts, offenders on probation or parole, court proceedings involving domestic matters, notably divorce cases, disputes over guardianship of children, wills and unusual forms of religious practices.

Taking the complaints about the press from all sources, we can broadly summarise the objections as follows. In acquiring news, some of the press are said to have obtained entry to private premises and to have conducted interviews by deception; and to have pestered and otherwise harassed people in private places, which was all the more objectionable when the news itself was distressing to those harassed. In publishing news and comment, they are said to have made known, mainly to satisfy idle curiosity, facts which would otherwise be generally unknown, about private misfortunes, calamities and other incidents, so aggravating the distress or embarrassment; or to have published, with critical innuendo, stories about unusual but lawful private activities and behaviour which are judged to be objectionable to current conventional opinion: and in all these situations to have identified directly or indirectly the individuals concerned. These practices, it is claimed in the critical evidence presented to us, can do grave damage to private individuals, out of proportion to any general benefit derived from the dissemination of the news.

... The West Sussex County Council in a public statement said that the reunion of a foster child with its natural parents 'is something which has to be done gently and quietly and privately. This was impossible in this case because the situation was manipulated by the national press for their own circulation motives and entirely regardless of the feelings of the people concerned.' In a letter to us the Clerk to the Council added that 'it is virtually impossible to make a calm and objective decision regarding a child's future when all the parties involved are being subjected to the very considerable stresses of the "news" media.' Elsewhere he said: 'There was no question of the press doing public good by highlighting the irregularities of a local authority and no one could honestly argue that the publicity given could in any way be in [the foster child's] interests.'

The argument seems to run that it was not necessary for the public discussion of the important social issues involved in fostering policy to publish photographs or vivid accounts of the children in their confusion and unhappiness, which may have left a lasting psychological impression on them. Against this it was claimed that it was precisely the vivid descriptions and photographs of the children's distress and bewilderment which effectively conveyed to the public the real depth of the emotions involved and stimulated public interest in a social issue of importance.

. . . It has been put to us that publicity given in a person's local paper to some minor offence, such as petty theft in a supermarket or drunkenness, possibly committed well outside the locality, adds a further penalty, such as loss of employment or local ridicule and ostracism, out of all proportion to whatever penalty the magistrates may have imposed. It is argued that this is a haphazard additional penalty: firstly, because its effect on someone living in a small community like a village is likely to be much stronger than in a more anonymous urban setting; secondly, because its effect on people in some walks or stations of life can be far more damaging than on others; thirdly, because the decision to publish will depend on the particular editor's normal practice or shortage of news, or even whim; and fourthly, because the magistrates may or may not have taken account of the possible effect of publicity in fixing the sentence: some do, we are told, and others do not. Such haphazard consequences, it is argued, must result in injustice.

A former schoolmaster told us that he had been dismissed from his teaching post because of the publicity given to a conviction for a minor sexual offence, despite the fact that the Department of Education and Science had ruled that he was not an unfit person to teach. It is the opinion of those who are concerned about the damage which is done to individuals that to give publicity to cases such as this is not warranted on grounds of importance. They say that, if such cases become important because of frequency, public knowledge of their incidence, and thereby increased precautions against them, does not depend on knowing also the identities of the offenders.

However, the Younger Committee concluded that such intrusions on privacy were adequately dealt with by the Press Council, a non-statutory body which has powers to consider complaints and to issue rebukes when it considers them justified. The Committee found:

40B Younger Report
THE PRESS COUNCIL

The Press Council operates therefore on a fairly large scale and is experienced in dealing with complaints from the public. The number of these which concern privacy is, however, a tiny proportion of the whole. In the whole period from the Council's inception in 1953 up to 30 June 1970 a total of only 65 privacy cases were adjudicated upon, of which 37 were upheld and 28 rejected. The annual average number of cases adjudicated upon was thus three and a half, with two cases upheld and one and a half rejected. The three cases in the twelve months ending June 1970 concerned a complaint about the publication of the memoirs of Miss Christine Keeler, which was upheld, and two complaints about publication of the identities of those involved in heart transplants, both of which were rejected.

The Committee recommended that the Press Council should alter its make-up so that half of its members should come from outside the newspaper industry, and should codify its rulings on privacy to provide future guidance.

In the sphere of television, the Committee looked into the use of techniques of intrusion of the kind described earlier in this book:

40C Younger Report
USE OF RECORDING TECHNIQUES

The BBC told us that it treated the question involved in using its equipment surreptitiously as a moral problem; and that it used the technique 'on a few occasions in order to expose malpractices of unsocial behaviour, the view having been taken that the seriousness of the ill so exposed justifies a technique in itself repugnant . . . There may be . . . a category of anti-social behaviour which, while not strictly illegal, is so strongly at variance with accepted standards that to expose it, using unorthodox methods if necessary, is a valid function of a public service broadcasting organisation.' The BBC described the equipment which, although in daily use for all other forms of recording, could be used for surreptitious techniques if authority were given: telephoto lenses, radio microphones and pocket transmitters, parabolic microphones and miniature tape recorders. We have referred above to the BBC's internal directive on this subject. This was issued in 1967 by the then Director General of the BBC, Sir Hugh Greene, and is still in force. It does not forbid the use of surreptitious techniques, but directs that the assent of the Director of Public Affairs and the Editor of the News and Current Affairs must be obtained before using them. They would take their decision on the basis of the criterion set out at the beginning of this paragraph and also of the importance of the material and the inability to get it by any other means. Sir Hugh Greene had expected to be informed of all requests by programme staff to use these techniques and his successor, we were told, has since made this a specific requirement. The BBC told us also that only four requests had been received and that none had been granted: 'The association of the top levels of management with any decision to proceed is a guarantee that they will not be lightly used.'

. . . The Independent Television Companies Association (ITCA) confirmed that hidden devices had only rarely been used by independent television companies and mentioned three cases, additional to those above, all of which occurred prior to the 1968 ruling: first, of recording a telephone conversation about breaking the economic sanctions on Rhodesia; second, of recording a telephone conversation with a drug-trafficker; and, third, of filming and recording a taxi driver at London Airport who was said to be overcharging. Such methods, said the ITCA, should be used only as a last resort. In fact, we

received no complaints about independent television pro-
grammes.

The Committee concluded:

40D Younger Report
RESPONSIBILITIES OF BROADCASTING
AUTHORITIES

Bearing in mind what we have said above about the awareness
of their responsibilities with regard to privacy which has been
shown both by the Board of Governors of the BBC and by the
Members of the ITA, together with the insignificant number of
complaints which have been made against either body about
their handling of privacy matters, we conclude that no case has
been made out, on grounds of protection of privacy, for imposing on the Broadcasting Authorities any external control beyond
the laws generally applicable to all citizens.

SOURCE: *Report of the Committee on Privacy,* 1972

PRIVATE EYES
*The development of modern techniques of intrusion has led to a good
deal of anxiety about the activities of private detective agencies. In its
written evidence to the Younger Committee, the National Council for
Civil Liberties stated:*

41 NCCL
INTRUSION BY PRIVATE DETECTIVES

EJP Publications (James Pike Ltd) operate from an address in
St. Ives, Cornwall. Among other activities they offer a complete
correspondence course, in 14 lessons, on becoming a private
detective. Their literature is aimed at the absolute beginner
who wants to make an income either part-time or full-time, in
this very specialised profession.

Applicants are invited to start off in a modest way, operating from their own homes with only a telephone and a car as basic equipment. From this point, step by step they can build up an organisation to trace missing persons, handle divorce cases, make observations and private enquiries and debt recovery, provide personal escorts, serve process, deal in status enquiries and operate security service.

No capital is needed, no previous experience, no licence. It is a game anyone can play, and there is no shortage of persons looking for some extra money. Ex-convicts, unstable personalities, people with a taste for prying; anyone can join in.

It is the NCCL's view that all forms of intrusion into people's private lives are inherently undesirable. Some of them may be necessary, and in an industrial society we have to concede more than we would readily wish. But we find it wholly deplorable that there should be no control over who can carry out these tasks and under what conditions. Even a beginner can quickly master enough basic law to keep out of trouble, and very soon he will be assessing the ratio of risk to income in the use of devices like bugging and telephone tapping. It will not be long before he calculates the degree of threat and intimidation which may be applied in any given circumstances, and if he is unscrupulous enough he will apply it, since the rewards are high enough to make it worth his while.

William Noble, formerly of Scotland Yard and now a private detective operating in Benfleet, confirmed this warning. He mentioned the strict requirements of ABD members, but was concerned about some of the individuals outside the Association. 'As things stand,' he wrote, 'a villain can leave prison and open up a private detective agency without let or hindrance. At the moment there are several agencies operated by principals who have criminal records, one of whom advertises a lot for the specific purpose of catching mugs to well and truly fleece. And some of them are actually receiving assignments from solicitors!'

. . . One of the more questionable areas in which detective

agencies are sometimes asked to pry is the vetting of employees'
wives. The concept of a wife as an extension of her husband's
job is held by many corporations and firms. If his work requires
his presence at functions and entertainments, he tends to be
judged by his wife's habits. If his job has a security aspect, his
wife is often subjected to some form of discreet screening.

Peter Merken of the Ace Detective Agency put the matter
thus: 'You can tell a lot about a woman if you put a week's
surveillance on her and her house, watching all the comings and
goings for 16 hours a day.' Of course, he added, it is all done
very discreetly. Her birth, school, marriage and criminal records, if any, are tracked down. An agent with an extrovert
personality might pose as a salesman or a poll-taker, and talk
his way into her house.

The ubiquitous Barrie Quartermain takes up the story: 'We
have to make an assessment of the wife's personality . . . her
political leanings, and anything else that shows what she's like.
Sometimes we send an agent along with a genuine market
researcher who has a list of questions ranging from the wife's
taste in music, food and the arts to the number of times she has
sex with her husband every week.' It is Quartermain's boast
that, if the company is prepared to pay for it, 'we can even tell
them where the wife's birthmarks are. Three under the left
breast—that's a thorough search.'

. . . A final example is of the service offered by one unusually
audacious operator. David Read is the managing director of
the Capital Bureau of Investigations, and carries out his
business from an office in Teddington, Middlesex.

Read claims that he can obtain and supply secret information
about any citizen at the following prices:

    Bank balance, full details: 6 gns.
    Criminal record: 4 gns.
    Latest address from bank records: 5 gns.
    Ex-directory telephone number: 4 gns.
    An address for that telephone number: 4 gns.

A forwarding address left with the Post Office: 5 gns.
Traffic offences record: 3 gns.
Driving licence record: £2.12.6d.

Maintaining that he was 'supplying a needed service', Read
refused to divulge his source of information. He stated in a
circular that the Law Society offered no objection. At the time
this was true, for the very simple reason that the Law Society
had had no communication from the firm, and had conse-
quently been given no opportunity to object or not.

SOURCE: NCCL evidence to the Younger Committee

In 1971, The Guardian *tried the experiment of asking detective
agencies to investigate two members of its staff. (The two journalists
knew what was happening, but the agencies didn't know that they knew.)
One of them, Peter Harvey, reported:*

42A Peter Harvey
A PRIVATE INVESTIGATION EXPERIMENT

Confidential information on individual citizens is being systematically obtained from Government files and from banks for
commercial interests, foreign embassies, and private inquiry
agencies. Tax records, bank statements, Social Security files—
and more—are being secured through exploitation of leakages.

Some of the information is being supplied by Government
employees, some through retired employees, and some is
secured by confidence tricks. The same methods are used to
obtain information about companies.

Following allegations about the census, the Guardian has
made its own inquiry into the ease with which private information can be obtained. None of our inquiries relate to the census,
but they have shown that information can be obtained from the
Inland Revenue, the Social Services Ministry, banks, local
government departments, and the Motor Vehicle Registry.

K

Two private inquiry companies with which the Guardian was put in touch claimed to be able to secure important commercial information also from the Department of Trade and Industry, the Ministry of Transport and other sources. These claims and some of the background were put to an authority on Government security, with long experience but now no longer in Government service, and in his view the claims were almost certainly valid.

The system used to obtain information is complicated, but it can work speedily. To test the inquiry companies' capability, the first company was asked for information on two members of the Guardian's staff—myself and the news editor. In my own case confidential details were obtained from a local government office in less than 10 minutes.

A detailed dossier on the news editor was compiled and supplied within 48 hours, involving items from the Inland Revenue, the Department of Social Security, two banks, a vehicle licence office, and a rating office. It should be added that although the information was nearly all accurate it contained two errors.

In the second set of tests—made to make sure that information was coming from within Government departments and not only from non-Government sources—an inquiry company was asked for the earnings and income tax of a senior member of the staff who does not use an accountant for his tax return. A correct statement of last year's earnings, including freelance earnings as returned for tax, was supplied four days later. The earnings of the man's wife, as returned for tax, were also reported but with a £20 error which suggested a telephone mishearing.

In the second test the inquiry company was also asked to discover details of a named individual's dealings with a branch of the Home Office. This, although it seemed a severe test, was successfully accomplished. Confidential details previously unknown to the Guardian were supplied and have since been verified.

. . . Middlemen play a significant rôle. According to informants in the business, experienced civil servants are sometimes recruited from their Ministries on or before retirement. Many have valuable knowledge of departmental affairs and planning. These men are permitted to take post-retirement employment that is not usually allowed in other countries such as the United States and Germany. Steps are not always taken to ensure that when a man leaves a Ministry he does not take with him valuable up-to-date information.

People involved in obtaining information for us said that they 'regularly, four or five times a week' use the leak system to 'get details' of people and work from Government departments. The Inland Revenue, the Home Office, the Department of Trade and Industry, and the Aliens Registration Office were named.

On the non-industrial, non-diplomatic side, two main methods are used. 'A number of middlemen have set up business,' we were told. 'These are former employees of Government departments. They leave the Civil Service and then let it be known they are willing, for a price, to supply information to firms such as ours.

'We usually pay these people from about £2 to £8 per assignment. Usually it takes them only one quick phone call. Should we need, for example, to find out a man's or a company's taxation return we will contact the former Inland Revenue employee. He knows the departmental ropes and is able to call the right department of Inland Revenue—or Social Services, or the Home Office or whatever—and by talking in departmental language, giving the names of forms and the numbers of files he wants and by pretending to be so-and-so from such-and-such a branch, he invariably gets the information he is after. Or he can simply use the "old-boy" net. But that is not done very much; it is the first method that is used in eight cases out of 10.'

. . .'One can usually adopt a fairly effective cover story. Pretending to be someone in another branch of the same department and having some knowledge of say, the number of the form containing the information we are seeking. We find that time and time again we can obtain detailed information over the telephone from Government departments that really should not be divulged to anyone at all, let alone a voice on the phone. But it does happen. This approach, by the way, works especially well with local government departments.'

SOURCE: *The Guardian* (11 May 1971)

In 1973, Mr Ian Withers, head of a detective agency, and three of his colleagues were convicted of conspiracy because of their methods. Mr Withers, asserting that he had done nothing which was not normal in his profession, appealed, was released on bail, and continued his activities pending the hearing of the appeal. The Guardian *assigned Peter Harvey to sum up the case:*

42B Peter Harvey
EXPOSURE OF A PUBLIC MISCHIEF

The four people who stood in the dock of No. 4 over the past three weeks were charged with 'conspiring together to effect a public mischief by unlawfully obtaining private and confidential information from certain banks and building societies . . .' and with 'obtaining private and confidential information from certain departments of Government and local government.'

At one point, two days were to be spent in legal argument on just what constituted 'a public mischief,' but in the opening statement for the prosecution, Mr Michael Corkery went straight to what—for the vast majority of people outside that court—was the essence of the matter: private citizens, he said, had every right to believe that information in such places as the Criminal Records Office, the Inland Revenue, Social Security and NHS offices, banks, building societies and passport and alien registration offices would be kept secret.

Mr Corkery said that if the information was easily available to unauthorised people, it could lead to blackmail. He said the four defendants attempted to obtain confidential information

by 'lies and misrepresentation' and that they freely advertised
that their private inquiry agency could draw on the services of
informants inside Government departments.

What did the court hear . . . from witnesses, policemen and
the defendants themselves during a case described by the judge
on the opening day as one of great importance?

The private inquiry agency found some bank managers 'very
cooperative' in helping the agency to trace debtors. Mr Ian
Withers said he posed as a bank employee to trace debtors for
his clients; he 'chatted up' bank managers after saying he came
from another branch. '. . . those who were cooperative were
usually very cooperative.'

During the trial, bank security officers admitted they had no
real way of preventing confidential information being given out
to telephone callers; the Home Office admitted it had given
information to the inquiry agency; a firm of solicitors and the
manager of a finance company had asked for, and been given,
highly confidential information held by Government departments about clients—and a price list of services offered by the
detective agency, ranging from bank balances through to
criminal records, was read out.

SOURCE: *The Guardian* (10 February 1973)

The Younger Report confirms this disturbing picture:

43A Younger Report
PRIVATE INVESTIGATORS

The only organisations of which we are aware are the Association of British Investigators and the Association of British
Private Detectives. The Association of British Investigators has
a United Kingdom membership of 340 (plus an overseas
membership of 143). It is limited by guarantee and was in-
corporated on 31 December 1970 . . . The Association of

British Private Detectives has not made known its membership to us and failed to respond to our request for further information to establish its status. The Association of British Investigators runs a monthly journal called 'The Investigator' and the agencies it represents appear to be small concerns. As to the total number of persons operating as private detectives, we have heard of estimates ranging from 'between 15,000 and 20,000'—given in a BBC radio programme in September 1970—to 1,000, a figure given to us informally by a senior police officer. Although we have no hard evidence, on the basis of all that we have learned from a number of sources, we think that a reasonable estimate of the maximum number is of the order of 3,000.

Anyone can become a private detective and we have heard of one firm in Cornwall which offers a fourteen-lesson correspondence course for would-be private detectives, which is aimed at the complete beginner. The more reputable ones, at least, appear to be recruited from among former police officers, solicitors' clerks and ex-servicemen with experience of security work, but there is nothing to stop criminals who are at large from becoming private detectives.

Anyone with a knowledge of what to do can set up in the business from his home, if he has a telephone and preferably a car. Some private detectives resort to impersonation in order to get what they want, posing as police officers, social security officials, insurance men, market researchers, telephone engineers, journalists, factory inspectors or prospective employees. Some plant agents as a means of access to industrial and commercial premises. Some succeed in obtaining information from banks about their customers. They also obtain information publicly available from the General Register Office, the Principal Probate Registry, the Public Record Office, the Register of Electors, the Registrar of Companies and the Registrar of Shipping.

The Younger Committee decided—citing a number of cases—that the law is strong enough to deal with 'reprehensible practices'. But it was concerned over the situation which permits anyone to go into this business, and recommended a licensing system:

43B Younger Report
REPREHENSIBLE PRACTICES

Several court cases in recent years show how it has been possible effectively to invoke the criminal law against private detectives:

1. In September 1967 a private detective was convicted at Feltham, Middlesex, of offences against the Wireless Telegraphy Act 1949 for installing a wireless transmitter in a private telephone and using the transmitter without a licence. He was fined £150 and £100 on these counts respectively. He had gained access to the telephone by masquerading as a telephone engineer.

2. In February 1969 two enquiry agents were charged with conspiracy to effect a public mischief in connection with attempts to trace missing debtors by impersonating Inland Revenue officials. Both were found guilty and fined £5000 each: their company was fined £1000. Each was ordered to pay £300 costs and the company £50.

3. In June 1971 two private detectives were convicted at the Old Bailey for (a) conspiring together to contravene the Wireless Telegraphy Act 1949 and (b) conspiracy to trespass, while attempting to obtain evidence for use in a divorce case, by installing and using unlicensed radio transmitters. They were each sentenced to nine months' imprisonment (suspended for three years) and were each fined £300 and ordered to pay £250 costs.

4. In October 1971 a woman private detective and her employer, the proprietor of a private detective agency, were convicted at Lincoln Assizes of conspiring to get confidential information by corrupt means and to offer a bribe in order to obtain 'secret' information from a cer-

tain chemical firm. One was fined £100 and the other
£1500 on the first charge and each was fined a nominal
£1 on the second.

5. In February 1972 four private detectives were committed
for trial at the Central Criminal Court charged with
conspiring to obtain confidential information from banks
and Government records.

In the light of these cases we conclude that the law is at
present adequate to deal with the flagrantly reprehensible
practices of private detectives . . .

The work of private detectives is of exceptional concern to us
because invasion of privacy is the essence of it. If privacy is to be
given greater protection it would, on the face of it, seem necessary to have special regard to persons or organisations who hold
themselves out to invade privacy for reward. In spite of the
general good character of most British private detectives and of
the useful and even rather dull work they do, we have concluded
that there should be some special control over them. We have
been mainly influenced by the following factors. First, the proof
in a number of court proceedings that certain private detectives
have deliberately broken the law to pursue their activities;
second, the clear temptation to private detectives to take advantage for their private ends of the opportunities given to
them; third, the fact that even where the present law can be
invoked effectively, it is apparently an inadequate deterrent on
its own, as persons convicted of offences committed in the course
of inquiry work are free to resume their activities in the same
line of business; and fourth, the considered opinion of the
police, expressed in their formal memorandum of evidence,
that, because of the present complete lack of control, there are
ex-criminals and associates of criminals operating as private
detectives. We also note the desire of the Association of British
Investigators—apparently the only large organisation of private
detectives in this country—to have a licensing system.

. . . We were unable to discover to what extent private detectives operate outside their home locality, but we know that the larger agencies pursue their activities over a wide area, in effect countrywide, and we have no evidence to suggest that smaller agencies or single operators confine their activities to a narrow area. We have some reason to believe that most of the larger agencies are based in London. As we have noted above, some private investigations are commissioned by overseas Governments and other external organisations. In our view, therefore, it would be entirely appropriate that the supervision of private detectives should be central. We recommend accordingly that machinery be established, in whatever way the Government considers most efficient and economical, for a central licensing authority.

SOURCE: *Report of the Committee on Privacy* (1972)

THE BANKS

In certain respects, a man's bank manager knows more about his private affairs than anyone else—sometimes more than his wife. Confidence in the discretion of banks is traditional, at least in Britain. The Younger Committee was therefore much disturbed by the Guardian *experiment (42A, 42B), which showed that banks were among the institutions easily tapped for information by private detectives. The Younger Report says:*

44A Younger Report
INFORMATION SUPPLIED BY BANKS

We quoted this evidence to the Committee of London Clearing Bankers, who said they found it difficult to believe that any bank employee would answer questions about salary over the telephone. It was contrary to all instructions given by the banks to their staff, which were 'hammered home at every instructional course which every member of the staff attends at bank training centres'. They added: 'It is one of the first principles that any member of the staff realises, absolute secrecy of any information in that branch bank.' We were told that enquiries over the telephone were discouraged and that where, in urgent cases, they were accepted steps were taken (such as telephoning back) to ensure that the enquiry emanated from another bank.

We were not able to examine the enquiry agents who made these investigations, but what we were told left us in no doubt that information was obtained, possibly by deception, by people who had no right to have it and to whom a bank ought not to have supplied it. We take the view that no security system in this field can be completely foolproof, but we are disturbed by the apparent ease of penetration in this case. We believe that our proposals for control over private detectives . . . will, if implemented, reduce the likelihood of this sort of information being obtained in such a way, but meanwhile we strongly urge the banks to look to the arrangements they have for protecting the details of their clients' accounts in the interest of individual privacy and of public confidence in British banking practice.

Another question arose in connection with banks. How easy is it to find out the state of a customer's credit? And, equally disquieting perhaps, does the customer know that someone else is finding out? The Younger Committee reported:

44B Younger Report
CUSTOMERS' CREDITS AND BANKERS' REFERENCES

An obvious source of information about the credit-worthiness or financial commitments of individuals or companies is the bank holding their account and those who seek credit often explicitly authorise a potential grantor of credit to seek information about them from that source. The banks assured us that they considered themselves under a legal obligation not to disclose their customers' affairs without authority and that they were conscious of the importance of confidentiality in the relationship. It is possibly not widely known, however, that it is the practice of banks to give to other banking institutions, in response to enquiries on behalf of their customers, confidential opinions as to the credit-worthiness, reliability and standing of those who bank with them. We were told that such opinions were expressed in conventional and general terms and only to a carefully controlled list of organisations. The banks' view is that, where the customer's express consent is lacking, his consent is implied by the fact of maintaining the account, as the practice is a well-established service available to all customers. In providing this information a bank does not act in the same way as a credit agency, because the information conveyed is the branch manager's personal and confidential opinion on a customer's financial position as assessed by him on the basis of the records of the bank. Unlike banks, credit agencies have no relationship, legal or commercial, with the individuals on whom they report.

In 1969 the Consumers Association (CA) conducted an experiment in which a member of their staff asked her bank manager for a 'banker's reference' on a colleague, whose bank she named, in connexion with 'a proposed obligation of the order of £25 per month'. She received a reply that her colleague was 'highly respectable, of good standing and may be considered entirely trustworthy in the way of business' for such a commitment. The subject of this report was never told that an enquiry had been made and the CA suggested that if this experience was standard practice anyone could find out a bank's opinion of any of its customers with ease and so breach the traditional confidential relationship.

In the December 1971 issue of *Money Which?* CA reported the results of a similar experiment:

Money Which? has checked on the system [of bank references] by getting 15 people to ask for bank references on 15 other people —with the latter's consent—concerning entirely mythical transactions. The 30 people involved all had accounts with the Big Four banks.

All our enquiries were given a reference, and in none of these cases, did the bank manager tell the person being inquired about what was happening.

We also arranged for bank references to be sought on a small number of people who—because of their incomes, job or public position—might perhaps have expected extra privacy. Again, our inquirers got their references, and our top people were not told that references were being given about them—so status does not seem to give you any greater immunity.

Incidentally, most of the people who took part in our test had not realised that inquiries could be made by private individuals, and were surprised that such inquiries could be made without their knowledge.

CA recommend that banks should not give references unless the customer who is the subject of the reference has agreed in writing. The Association thought that this should be easy to arrange at little cost. For example, in formal transactions involving, say, applications for credit, the form could—in the part asking for the bank's name and address—include a tear-off slip giving specific authorisation to the bank to provide a reference.

The Committee of London Clearing Bankers told us that, provided details of the balance of account or of moneys paid in were not revealed, they saw no objection to the provision of references in the general terms used in the CA experiment. As to the implied consent of a customer to the provision of information, they relied upon the judgment in *Tournier v. National Provincial and Union Bank of England* to support the view that a reference in such terms was not a breach of the customer-bank relationship. Since the matter had never been tested definitely in the courts, however, the banking world would welcome a clarification of the position.

We asked if there would be any objection to notifying a customer when an enquiry was made about his financial standing or even expressly seeking his consent before answering it. We were told that this might damage the relationship between the customer, whether an individual or a company, and the enquirer. It was explained that a bank would be reluctant to say, even in reply to a direct enquiry from a customer, whether or not it had supplied information. If it became the practice to tell customers, the bankers' representatives thought that the number of enquiries would certainly diminish.

We doubt whether there is any serious or widespread abuse of the bank reference system, but we do not believe that the practice is as well-known and accepted among customers, particularly individuals, as the banks assert. Nor are we convinced that it would be undesirable for a customer to know what enquiries had been made about him and what replies had been given. On the contrary, we think the present situation is undesirable. We recommend that the banks should make clear to all customers, existing or prospective, the existence and manner of operation of their reference system, and give them the opportunity either to grant a standing authority for the provision of references or to require the bank to seek their consent on every occasion.

SOURCE: *Report of the Committee on Privacy*, 1972

CREDIT AND DEBT

Buying on credit is a practice that increases from year to year, and has lately received a further impetus with the proliferation of Access Cards, Barclaycards and so forth. Quite often, lenders and vendors are content to trust the borrower on the strength of a few facts about his job and salary or the value of his freehold house. But it is not at all rare for them to make further inquiries; and, lacking the time to do so themselves, they call on the services of credit rating agencies, which perform the same function in this sphere as private detectives. More than half the adult population of the United States is on file with such an agency, and Britain, though a good way behind, is moving in the same direction. Investigations made by credit rating agencies touch inevitably on privacy, and were a natural field for the attention of the Younger Committee:

45A Younger Report
CREDIT RATING AGENCIES

We received about 20 letters from members of the public and a few from small businesses about the operation of organisations concerned with credit rating and its adjunct, debt collecting. Different types of activity were complained of, but it was possible to group them into several broad categories: the difficulty encountered by an individual refused credit in discovering the grounds of the refusal; a fear that information about debts would become widely available; a suspicion that such organisations had access to Government records, such as those of the Inland Revenue; the use of private detectives and unscrupulous debt collectors by credit rating agencies; the information-seeking activities of particular firms; and a vague unease at newspaper reports of the purchase by credit rating agencies of copies of the electoral register on a massive scale and of the possible computerisation of their records.

. . . The original role of credit rating agencies was to collect information and to draw up credit registers recording facts about customers' credit-worthiness. Many of them now also undertake the collection of debts. All work on the basis of inviting firms—usually retailers—to pay a subscription to become 'members'. Members are invited to provide information about their experience in dealing with customers and are entitled on payment of a fee (although some subscriptions may provide for a limited free service) to information on the credit-worthiness of people with whom they contemplate doing business. The two major agencies are British Debt Services (BDS) and the United Association for the Protection of Trade (UAPT), who provide a nation-wide service. Nearly all the other agencies cover limited areas. Many of them belong to the National Association of Trade Protection Societies (NATPS). Most agencies (including UAPT and the present members of NATPS) are non-profit-seeking and do not provide information to non-members.

BDS and some smaller agencies operate on a normal commercial basis.

BDS has its head office in Manchester and regional offices in Birmingham, Glasgow, Leeds, Liverpool, London, Newcastle and Nottingham. It has some 2500 subscribers or members and its files contain about 8 million items of information less than seven years old, covering the whole of the United Kingdom (as several items are often recorded against one name the number of names recorded is less than this). The principal contents of the files include:

a. all registered county court judgments, of which there were over 500,000 in 1969; this information is publicly available on payment;
b. unregistered county court judgments under £10 obtained as a result of a court action by BDS;
c. trade information supplied by members about items such as bad debts and repossessions;
d. bankruptcy proceedings;
e. bills of sale;
f. deeds of arrangements;
g. satisfactions of judgments and bills of sale;
h. decrees granted by Scottish Sheriff Courts;
i. estates sequestered;
j. trust deeds granted;
k. changes of address of known debtors.

The registered county court judgments referred to in a. above are those for £10 or more which have not been satisfied within one month of judgment being given or where notice of appeal has been given. A consumer can therefore contest a disputed debt without risk of his name appearing on the registers provided that, if he loses his case, he pays within one month. BDS is the only agency having a central national credit reference bureau. It deals with enquiries from mail order businesses, hire-purchase and rental organisations, public utilities, credit card companies, multiple retailers and check traders and is currently answering enquiries at the rate of over 4 million a year. The regional offices give oral reports by telephone and have access to the national bureau service. Because of the credit squeeze enquiries declined in 1969, but the 1970 figures show an upward trend which seems likely to have been continued in the 1971 figures. During 1969 the accounts collection service recovered over £1,500,000. Like most credit agencies BDS does not make recommendations about the granting of credit. It reports the facts and leaves the enquirer to decide what action to take. BDS is also willing to search electoral registers to find out whether a potential customer resides at the address he has given. This is of particular help to firms contemplating extending credit.

UAPT is a non-profit-seeking organisation which has worked in the credit reporting and accounts collection field for over a century. It has about 12,000 members. UAPT, unlike BDS, does not maintain a central national register. It maintains records at each of its offices and, in considering the opening of branches, tries to strike a balance between the desirability of providing a local service and the need to avoid fragmentation of records. The present registers of UAPT were formed in 1964 by the amalgamation of the registers originally maintained by the Association and by Kemps Mercantile Offices. UAPT has subsequently taken over a number of small credit agencies and opened some additional branches. At present it has 39 offices (with three more in preparation) and we understand that the Association's present view is that 50 offices would provide an optimum service.

The register in the various offices records on cards information about 14 million people; about 10,000 additional items (not all involving new names) are added daily to the record. Practice is not uniform between offices. Cards are generally kept in alphabetical order by name, except in the Inner London office, where they are indexed alphabetically by address, and in the Liverpool and Manchester offices, in each of which there is a second register by street. Entries (except bankruptcies) are deleted after six years unless the cards bear later information. It is understood that UAPT considered computerisation of the records but found it uneconomic at the present time since the capital cost would be at least £2 million and the running costs of lines linking branches with a central computer would also be heavy.

. . . We asked ourselves the question: are there any types of information about an individual which should never be recorded by a credit rating agency? In attempting to answer this we distinguished between information that was publicly available (such as the electoral register or county court judgments) and that which was not. We can see no reason why credit bureaux should not record as part of their business information available in public documents. As to other information, the question arises most sharply in connection with status reporting, which we consider next.

The provision to their members by some credit register agencies of so-called status reports on both individuals and companies is a more contentious practice than the recording of publicly available information. These reports involve local enquiries either by the agency's own employees or by 'correspondents' or enquiry agents. In some cases the enquiry agents are private detectives, many of whom do this sort of work as an adjunct to matrimonial enquiries. We were told by BDS that it no longer provides this service:

A status report commonly means an investigative report containing opinions and comments obtained through interviews. BDS inaugurated a research programme to investigate this area of credit reporting in an effort to eliminate a large element of guesswork and hearsay evidence which has always been associated with this type of report. It was apparent that status reporting in this country is based almost entirely on evidence gleaned from neighbours and local traders and only infrequently was a visit made to the home of the subject of the enquiry. Fears that unreasonable infringement of a right of privacy may take place by the recording by a credit bureau of this type of information which may be irrelevant to the granting

L

of credit are well founded. BDS has relied solely on factual information and does not intend to put its reputation at risk by introducing information which does not emanate from an official, public or reliable trade source. BDS provides information which is relevant only for the purpose of establishing a customer's eligibility for a consumer credit transaction or the collection of an overdue account. The files do not contain any information as to the character, general reputation or morals of an individual.

UAPT, however, provides status reports to members on request, mainly on business concerns. The situation with these differs from that in relation to individuals, because larger sums of money are usually involved, speed is of less importance and the possibilities of enquiries (from suppliers, the Companies' Register and so on) enable a more reliable service to be provided. Status reports on individuals are provided in the case of large transactions where little or no information is available on file. UAPT told us that it was not wholly happy about this area of its service, particularly in relation to individuals, and that it was being used less: the total number of reports per year dropped from 465,755 in 1966 to 371,227 in 1970, of which the majority related to commercial transactions.

There may be some cases where a retailer, faced with the possibility of losing a large sum of money, might require rather more information about a credit seeker than would normally be recorded by a credit bureau. We note that BDS as a matter of deliberate policy no longer provides status reports while UAPT still provides them on request. It seems to us that the practice of BDS in excluding from the material they hold 'any information as to the character, general reputation or morals of an individual' is the right one and we strongly recommend that UAPT and other credit rating agencies offering this service should voluntarily withdraw it. We believe that they would have a strong inducement to take this step if they knew that individuals reported on had a legal and well-publicised right of access to the agency report.

The Committee examined, but rejected, a plan proposed by Mr Leslie Huckfield, MP, for licensing and controlling credit rating agencies.

45B Younger Report
CONTROL OF INFORMATION BILL

Under the Control of Information Bill proposed by Mr Leslie Huckfield MP, a credit agency with records of over 100,000 individuals would be required to have a licence from a Data Bank Tribunal, a body designed to control the use of all large stores of information, whether or not computerised, in both the public and private sectors. The Tribunal would have power to require an agency to provide individuals regularly with a copy of their record and to permit them access to it at any time on payment of a fee, to say what classes of information should not be stored, to forbid the agency to supply 'certain persons or categories of persons' with information, and to require the destruction of information after a time. In short the Bill would deal with all those operations of agencies which we think should be looked at because of their actual or potential effect on individual privacy . . .

. . . But we believe that our recommendations for giving access to information held in credit registers and for controlling investigations made with a view to providing status reports will be sufficient to deal with the most important areas of anxiety . . .

As to Mr Huckfield's Bill we appreciate the great advantages of its approach: its flexibility, its comprehensiveness and its enforceability. But, as in many other areas of our investigation, we had to measure the restrictions on useful and harmless activities and the cost likely to result from legislation against the evil or in many cases the threat of evil which it was designed to combat. We were conscious of the fact that the information stores of credit agencies are only a small part of the 'data banks' that would be affected by the Bill; that it was designed to extend to an area outside our terms of reference; and that the evidence of abuse within those terms was negligible and could in our view be corrected by simpler measures than those proposed by Mr Huckfield. We therefore conclude that as far as credit registers are concerned legislation such as he proposed would be inappropriate.

SOURCE: *Report of the Committee on Privacy*, 1972

As the Younger Report notes, credit rating agencies also sometimes take on the job of collecting debts. Here, the invasion of privacy is often deliberate and is part of the technique of enforcing payment. Some examples were given in the NCCL's evidence to the Younger Committee:

46 NCCL
DEBT COLLECTING PROCEDURES

Manaton Central Register of Defaulters, Cromwell Road, London SW7

One of Manaton's methods of bringing defaulters into line is to write threatening that they will be 'blacklisted locally and nationally' unless payment is received. On one such occasion the recipient was withholding payment from a garage owing to dissatisfaction with work carried out. He could not, by any reasonable definition be regarded as a bad payer. But Manaton, a firm of whom he had never heard and with whom he had never had any dealings, were able with impunity to threaten him with draconian retribution.

Here is the threat. A man is listed as a 'bad-payer' merely on the word of Manaton's subscribers, who might be actuated by malice, or have made a mistake, or have failed to evaluate the data properly, or are simply in dispute with the customer. He will be entered on some blacklist of whose very existence he will not be aware, and might find himself on the receiving end of 'local and national' publicity, or be unable in the future to obtain credit.

Status Investigators Ltd., Piccadilly, London W1

A spokesman for this company has admitted that 'some element of threat, is necessary in dealing with default. He was reticent about what form such threat would ordinarily take, but suggests that, in its absence, 90% of debtors would simply take no notice.

Kentlaun Agencies, London

This firm normally calls at a debtor's home to collect payments, but will call at his place of employment if he proves unco-operative. In this event, they will ask his employer's permission, and reveal their purpose if asked to do so. Not surprisingly, they report that the debtor, after receiving such a visit, 'gets very co-operative and usually pays' . . .

Credit Default Register, Leeds

Causing embarrassment is also very much a part of the business of this company. A Salford man who owed a relatively small sum to the Midland Bank received a letter from Credit Default Register demanding immediate payment. The letter-heading contained a picture of a van bearing on its side, in bold letters: BAD DEBT COLLECTIONS. The letter contained the words: 'Our van will commence calling in 14 days if no reply is received within that time and if this causes you embarrassment you must consider it your own responsibility'.

Investigation & Trade Protection Bureau, London W1

A complaint was received by the NCCL from a lady in St. Albans. She received a letter addressed to 'The occupier' informing her that a Default Summons was pending against the person next door, and asking for confirmation that that person was still resident at that address. She complained strongly about such a high-handed action, which seemed expressly designed to publicise her neighbour's predicament.

This is one case that came to light only because 'the occupier' happened to be unusually public-spirited about a course of action aimed at someone else.

The NCCL invited the company to comment, but no satisfaction was obtained. This appears to be a regular procedure.

SOURCE: NCCL evidence to the Committee on Privacy

The Younger Report itself added to these examples:

47 Younger Report
DEBT COLLECTING PROCEDURES

Our attention was drawn to certain practices, not directly related to credit rating, but associated with the granting of credit, namely debt collecting. One correspondent told us that he had received a letter from a debt collecting firm who threatened to park a van marked 'Debt Collection Company' outside his house until an outstanding account of £8 was cleared. He would, the firm said, be charged for the expenses incurred by it in carrying out its threat. Other practices adopted by some debt-collecting agencies were reported by the John Hilton Bureau of the News of the World to the Payne Committee on the Enforcement of Judgment Debts and referred to in their report. As well as the behaviour of which our correspondent complained, these practices were reported to include:

    i. 'the blue frightener' i.e. a printed notice of intention to institute proceedings in a county court but printed in black letters on blue paper so as to simulate a county court summons;

    ii. 'the red frightener' i.e. a printed notice with large red letters on white paper under the rubric 'You have 4 days in which to reduce your debt';

    iii. frequent calls at the home of the debtor leaving threatening cards:

    iv. informing neighbours of the debtor about his indebtedness under the guise of seeking information;

    v. informing local shopkeepers of the indebtedness of the debtor under the guise of seeking information;

    vi. threatening to paint a motor car with the statement that it is the property of the creditor;

    vii. writing to the employer of the debtor about his indebtedness under the guise of avoiding the need for the debtor to absent himself from work to attend court.

SOURCE: *Report of the Committee on Privacy*, 1972

In 1970, soon after the Younger Committee began its inquiries, Parliament passed the Administration of Justice Act, including a section imposing penalties for this kind of harassment. The Committee took the view that it provided adequate protection. The NCCL, however, is of the opinion that it has had little 'bite'; it may well be that the harassed are unaware that they now have a remedy at law, or feel that a complaint would land them in precisely the publicity that they are anxious to avoid. This kind of intrusion on privacy, at all events, is likely to remain an unsolved problem.

GETTING A JOB

An employer choosing among applicants for a job is in a strong position —certainly if the job is desirable and if unemployment is prevalent— and it is well known from common experience that some employers take advantage of this position to ask questions that intrude on privacy and have no very obvious connection with the work to be done. If such questions were forbidden, employers would probably manage without them (some employers regularly discriminated on grounds of colour, but were not observed to go out of business when this was forbidden by the Race Relations Act). But the problem is a tricky one, and the Younger Committee recorded: 'We find it difficult to see how the amount and type of information an employer is allowed to seek could be restricted by statute.'

The Younger Report does, however, cast some light on the facts:

48 Younger Report
INFORMATION REQUESTED BY
PROSPECTIVE EMPLOYERS

We were shown in evidence a number of questionnaires which contained personal questions which did not seem to us to have anything to do with the type of employment sought. These included questions about height and weight at age 18, 20, 25, 30, 35, 40 and 45; about reading matter; and about family background and marital history ('date engaged; date married; date separated; date divorced; date remarried; date widowed'). The National Council for Civil Liberties sent us a copy of a questionnaire which required an applicant to say how many times a week he entertained in his own home and to name and give other details of friends in various categories of association with him. The TUC told us of a survey, undertaken by the Industrial Society, of 50 application forms used by different firms, which showed that employers obtained not only basic information such as age, sex, qualifications, but also details of marital status, numbers and ages of children, numbers and ages of brothers and sisters, other dependents, father's job, religion, relations or friends employed by the firm, right- or left-handedness, trade union membership, spare-time employment, driving licence endorsements and intelligence test results. The Employment Agents Federation told us that applicants for employment normally completed an application form and submitted to an interview of at least 20 minutes. An applicant would expect to give details of his education including any special training designed to fit him for a particular career and details of any educational programme he might have in mind for the future. The applicant's health might have to be discussed frankly since it could affect his ability to perform certain work or to work for long periods. His family position could be of consequence. 'Much of this information will be discarded but it is true to say that at the end of the interview the interviewer, and therefore the agency, will be in possession of a great deal of personal information about the applicant. Probably, in fact, more than the applicant himself realises.'

The TUC urged us to consider drawing up 'a list of questions which could be recommended as appropriate for use in normal circumstances'. They also suggested that we 'might usefully list the matters on which questions should not normally be asked'. The National Federation of Professional Workers said:

> It is clearly objectionable that any data recorded in reference to an individual's employment should contain any additional information which is entirely irrelevant to his employment. For instance, though employment particulars may be of relevance to credit rating, credit rating should be regarded as irrelevant to employment. Though employment is of profound importance to Inland Revenue, other aspects of a man's tax liability are not relevant to his employer.

SOURCE: *Report of the Committee on Privacy*, 1972

The National Council for Civil Liberties, in its evidence to the Committee, named a firm which asked applicants to state the value of their houses (if owned), their current monthly expenses, the nature and amount of their investments, and for how many months they could support themselves—this, by the way, was not even for a job but for employment as freelance salesmen. Another firm asked: 'Religion? Father's occupation? Are you an active member of any societies or clubs, with their names please?' And there is even a firm which asks: 'What was the last book you read? When? Do you read newspapers regularly? Which?'

A special problem arises with regard to men who have come out of prison, and have to reveal this to potential employers through the absence of stamps on their National Insurance cards. To find a way of eliminating this situation would surely be to strike a blow for privacy. But apparently employers can also gain knowledge of convictions which were well in the past and perhaps resulted only in a fine, for the Younger Report cites a correspondent who 'quoted the claim by the chief security officer of a large engineering works that he had contacts who could obtain details of criminal convictions'.

Relevant in this connection is a point made by Mr James B. Rule in his survey of the police records system:

49 James B. Rule
CRIMINAL RECORDS OF EMPLOYEES

Another point which the Home Office spokesmen pressed quite strongly at the time of our meeting was their insistence that employers are unable to obtain information from the police on the criminal records of prospective employees. The research has shown this assertion, too, to be faulty, although here the picture is more mixed. It is very common for employers to seek information from criminal records so as to exclude former criminals from employment, especially if the nature of the job is such as to make criminal behaviour by employees especially troublesome. The police, for their part, are quite varied in their attitudes towards such entreaties. Some police officials report providing such information readily under certain circumstances, while others flatly disclaim all such disclosure. Such variations no doubt correspond to differences of opinion concerning the ethics of such disclosure, with different members of the police following various policies under various circumstances.

It is by no means rare, for example, for the police to provide advice concerning job applicants to administrators of children's homes, or to headmasters of schools. This advice may entail merely a recommendation not to hire in specific cases, or it may involve more detailed disclosure of an applicant's past record of crimes against children. Police are probably more likely to cooperate here than elsewhere, because of special repugnance concerning these sorts of crimes, and because of their knowledge that persons with tendencies in this direction often actively seek employment in such institutions.

Perhaps less widespread is the provision of information to

other employers at special risk from theft or other criminal activity on the part of their employees. Some forces and criminal record offices routinely review lists of seasonal employment applicants at resorts and holiday camps in order to screen out those with convictions for larceny, breaking and entering, and the like. Similar requests for advice come regularly from banks and other firms whose employees must look after highly valuable and portable property. These, too, are honoured unevenly, and it is difficult to put any definite figure on the frequency with which the firms succeed in obtaining directly the information they seek.

There is reason to believe, however, that no employer with resources and patience need go without information of this kind. The police record-keeping system is, after all, an enormous bureaucratic mechanism designed to provide information on people's criminal records, a mechanism with numerous exits through which such information can flow. It is very difficult to prevent such a mechanism from working for unofficial as well as official purposes. Criminal record offices, for example, answer hundreds of telephone requests each day—the figure is in the thousands for the Metropolitan Office. The routine response to these requests is a report on some person's status in the wanted and missing index, and often a summary of his criminal record. It is impossible to prevent in all cases the dissemination of such information to non-police callers, even though criminal record office staffs may do their best to do so. Virtually anyone familiar with the telephone number of the regional office and the routines for making such requests can eventually obtain the information he seeks; if not on the first try, then sooner or later.

The vulnerability of these offices is especially great to former members of the police, who are invariably well versed in the techniques of making such requests. Industrial firms employ retired policemen in large numbers as security officers, precisely because of their familiarity with police routines in these and other matters. In many cases, too, the personal ties between these private security officers and their former colleagues make

it possible for them to obtain services which would be denied
to others.

SOURCE: James B. Rule. *Private Lives and Public Surveillance*
(1973)

STUDENTS AND PRIVACY

*Students occupy an in-between position in society, subject to less control
than school pupils but more than working adults (or working people of
equivalent age). University staff—tutors especially—inevitably acquire
a good deal of information about students. The question of privacy is
largely a question of how much of this information should be recorded,
how much should be passed on, and to whom. If embodied in a university
reference which the student carries when applying for his first job, it may
perhaps follow him through life.*

*All universities have files about their students—primarily a record of
courses studied and exam results—and in 1969 British universities
joined together to establish a computerised record of students, which is
maintained centrally on the computer belonging to the Universities
Central Council on Admissions (UCCA). It includes basic biographical
facts (age, sex, marital status, nationality, parent's occupation) plus a
record of academic progress, ending up with 'first employment'.*

*The Younger Report records that misgivings about this Statistical
Record were expressed by the National Union of Students and by the
Cambridge University Appointments Board:*

50 Younger Report
STATISTICAL RECORD OF STUDENTS

The NUS expressed misgivings about the Statistical Record,
which they regarded as a 'Government information scheme',
and said that they would find it acceptable only if an individual
were provided with an 'automatic' print-out (that is to say, not
merely on request). In addition 'inspection of the computer
programme by individuals should be allowed to ensure that the
print-out contains all the information stored in the computer'.
They suggested to us that the record should be subject to

scrutiny of coverage, methods and the uses made of the information by a statutory Committee of Parliament which should publish regular accounts of its findings on the lines of those published by the Public Accounts Committee.

The CUAB objected on grounds of principle to the linking of names with information about first employment of graduates because of the potential for misuse of such information, possibly by an autocratic and illiberal government. For this reason, we were told, Cambridge University originally declined to cooperate in the scheme. Later the CUAB told us that in March 1971 the Vice-Chancellors' Committee had accepted Cambridge University's contention and agreed to remove names from the record after the link had been made with the other data in it. The arrangement agreed was that names would be removed five years after the end of an undergraduate course or three years after the end of a graduate course. But the CUAB remained of the view that there was no need for the name of a student to be kept by UCCA once the student's entry process to a university had been completed. On the other hand the Standing Conference of Universities' Appointments Services, although they had taken exception, as early as September 1969, to the linking of names and data, were satisfied with the measures for assuring confidentiality. They feared rather that the very tightness of the control introduced over the records to protect their confidentiality would render it more difficult to obtain information to help assess 'graduate need and utilisation'.

SOURCE: *Report of the Committee on Privacy*, 1972

The Committee concluded that it would not be 'either impracticable or costly' to separate the names from the data, and advised the universities to 'review their policy on this matter'.

However, the files kept by some individual universities do not seem to be limited to basic facts. This became clear when, during a stormy period of student unrest, the archives were invaded and opened in

*the course of sit-ins. At the University of East Anglia, this was the
story:*

51 'The Guardian'
UNIVERSITY OF EAST ANGLIA'S
STUDENT DOCUMENTS

Students at the University of East Anglia, Norwich, have circulated documents which they claim prove that a campus
intelligence service has been set up.

The documents were taken from the office of the Dean of
Students, Dr John Coates, in March, when about a third of the
2,800 students staged a nine day sit-in at the university's
teaching building after the expulsion of a student convicted of
drug offences . . .

Although it is not an offence at the university for men and
women students to sleep together there are detailed memos
from officials telling Dr Coates of who was believed to be sleeping with whom. According to the memos, the main objection
was that cleaning staff were embarrassed at finding students in
bed together. Another memo informs Dr Coates of the addresses
of rented flats in Norwich in which men and women students
were believed to live together.

Mr Keva Coombes, president of the students' union, said
yesterday: 'The cohabitation memos are really rather laugh-
able, but I can't see that it was any business of Dr Coates.'

One series of documents includes a letter from Dr Coates to
a girl, thanking her for giving evidence against another girl and
assuring her that she would not be identified, but her name is
on the letter.

An accompanying statement from the girl gives details of
associates of the other girl, who was later given a suspended
'exclusion' for the possession of drugs. In his letter to the infor-
mant, Dr Coates regrets the leniency of the senate's disciplinary
committee.

Mr Coombs, a second-year history student from Broadstairs,
added: 'The university is very tense. We know that members of

the faculty are furious about the circulation of the document, but we are furious, too. We were assured last year, after the affair at Warwick University, that only admin files were kept on us. We now know that that was untrue.'

SOURCE: *The Guardian* (5 May 1971)

Dr Coates absolutely denied the construction put on the documents by the students, and stated that the university's only concern was to keep its record of lodgings and addresses in good order. The atmosphere of suspicion probably owed a great deal to a recent episode at Warwick University.

Letters found in the Warwick University files, and seized by the students, showed that the Vice-Chancellor, Dr J. B. Butterworth, was (to say the least) the recipient of information which raised crucial issues of privacy. There was, in the first place, a letter from a senior executive of Rootes Motors (now part of the Chrysler Group), a donor to the university, enclosing a report on a Labour Party meeting addressed by Professor Montgomery of Pittsburgh, then a visiting member of the Warwick University staff.

52A Warwick University files
REPORT OF A LABOUR PARTY MEETING
Report by N. P. Catchpole, Legal Adviser of the Rootes Organization, of the meeting of the Coventry Labour Party on 3 March 1969

Accompanied by Mr T. Norton, Security Officer, Stoke, I duly attended a meeting of the Coventry Labour Party at its offices on the evening of Monday 3 March.

The guest speaker, Dr D. Montgomery, spoke for about half an hour to an audience of eight people including the chairman who, incidentally, is an ex-Labour Councillor by the name of Edwards. I think that one member of the audience may have been Mr Bob Mitchell, one of the left-wing students at Warwick University. The remainder included Mr H. Finch, whom

I understand is a shop steward at Dunlops; with the exception of a shorthand writer who is on Norton's staff there were no other Rootes employees present.

Then there was some correspondence relating to an incident in which students had helped to hand out leaflets, on behalf of the Schools Action Union, to pupils of Kenilworth High School.

52B Warwick University files
LETTER TO THE CHAIRMAN OF THE
WARWICKSHIRE EDUCATION COMMITTEE

An unsigned letter from the University to Alderman H. H. C. Douty, Chairman of the Warwickshire Education Committee

Alderman H. H. C. Douty   2 December 1969
Northend
Dunchurch
Nr Rugby

Thank you very much for letting me know so quickly about the distribution of a pamphlet outside the Abbey High School in Kenilworth. I received this morning a copy of the paper which was being handed out. Of the three persons you mention, Judith Condon and Ann Freud are members of the University. I have turned up their records this morning and you may be interested to know that in each case the headmistress of the girl gave her an absolutely first-class reference. We have no recollection of the third, Julian Harber, having any connexion with the University. I am very distressed that this should have happened and have already spoken to the headmaster. If there are any further instances I hope I shall be informed.

As you may know, universities have no authority over students outside the University. By law they are adult at the age of eighteen and will shortly receive the vote. As I said on the telephone, a Vice-Chancellor has now by law no further influence over the outside activities of his students than the Managing Director of Rootes has over the outside activities of his employees. However, I greatly sympathise with the head-master. I would like to be kept informed and if I can see an opportunity for taking action you may be sure I will do so.

52C Warwick University files
MINUTES OF MEETING OF OFFICERS
OF COUNCIL

Extracts from the minutes of weekly meetings of Officers of Council (no date)

In the course of the meeting the Vice-Chancellor received a telephone call from Alderman Douty complaining that three girls had distributed leaflets outside the Kenilworth Abbey High School, calling a meeting of a 'Schools Action Group'. The girls, who were thought to be University of Warwick students, were named as Judith Condon, Ann Frued [sic] and Julianne [sic] Harber of 42 High Street, Kenilworth. It ap-peared that an angry parent had telephoned Mr Forsyth, who was Chairman of the Governors of the Kenilworth Abbey High School. The Vice-Chancellor pointed out that Mr Forsyth had defended the University when the question of the County Council grant was discussed, and he was anxious that the name of the University should not be brought into disrepute and the goodwill of the County Council lost. Alderman Douty, it was clear, expected some action to be taken. The problem of taking action over an incident outside the University, and not in con-travention of University regulations, was discussed. It was thought that the Vice-Chancellor might speak to Poulton about the incident, and possibly have a word with Mr Forsyth. . . .

The Registrar reported on the news from Essex about Julian Harber, the third person, presumably, to have distributed leaflets outside Kenilworth High School in December; it raised the question of whether he was qualified to take a higher degree

M

at Warwick. It was suggested that candidates from Essex might be carefully screened in future. The VC asked for a note on the whole Kenilworth incident. The AVC to talk to police about 42 High Street, Kenilworth.

But the item that became most famous was revealed by letters between a headmaster and the University about a sixth-former named Michael Wolf, who had applied for admission.

52D Warwick University files
LETTER FROM THE HEADMASTER OF WILLIAM ELLIS SCHOOL

From the Headmaster of William Ellis School to the Tutor for Admissions, Faculty of Science

The Tutor for Admissions   William Ellis School
Faculty of Science   Highgate Road
University of Warwick   London NW5
Coventry   17 February 1969

Strictly confidential

Dear Sir

Michael Wolf, Course No. 37220, Molecular Science

I write to you concerning the application for entry in 1969 of M. Wolf of this school. I find it necessary to add to the comments made on the UCCA entry form concerning his preoccupation with student politics. He is now a committee member of the London Schools Action Group, engaged in the organising of protests and demonstrations concerning school government, etc. His name appeared in *The Times Educational Supplement* of 10 January, expressing his intention to embark on militant action when necessary.

I felt it was important that you should be aware of this in making your decision. I would prefer this communication to be treated very confidentially, and should be pleased to receive your comments.

Yours faithfully
Sydney L. Baxter (signed)
Headmaster
(Written at foot of letter: **Reject This Man**, J.B.B. (signed).)

52E Warwick University files
LETTER TO THE HEADMASTER OF
WILLIAM ELLIS SCHOOL
From the Registrar to the Headmaster of William Ellis School

S. L. Baxter, MA   4 March 1969
Headmaster
William Ellis School
Highgate Road
London NW5

Personal

Dear Headmaster

I am writing to acknowledge your letter of 17 February, addressed to the Tutor for Admissions, regarding Michael Wolf. The Vice-Chancellor has asked me to say how very much obliged we were to you for writing in this way. We really are most grateful to you.

You may wish to know—privately—that the course selector has decided not to make an offer in this case. But it will no doubt be a week or two before the candidate hears of this officially through UCCA.

Yours sincerely
Registrar

SOURCE: E. P. Thompson (ed). *Warwick University Limite* (1970)

PART FOUR

Remedies

THE PRIVACY DEBATE

Privacy has been debated in the House of Commons on two recent occasions, in 1970 and in 1973. This is not very much, especially as both debates took place on Fridays when attendance is expected to be poor. However, under the British system of government, it is to Parliament that we must look for remedies when our privacy is invaded or threatened, so these debates are important and passages from certain speeches are well worth reading. We begin with the 1970 debate. Mr Brian Walden was introducing his Privacy Bill, and Mr James Callaghan was Home Secretary.

53A Brian Walden (Birmingham, All Saints, Labour)
PRIVACY BILL DEBATE

Whatever view one takes of the Bill, I do not think that anyone in the House has said or could say that Parliament has no concern about privacy and that people are indifferent to whether their privacy is protected. I make that point at the outset because, in certain fashionable intellectual circles, it is in vogue to hold a quite different view.

Thus it is that we have to endure the tedium of reading in print the pimples and problems of café society, and perhaps it is because of that that the feeling has grown up that, somehow, a longing for privacy is a remnant of a more savage existence, a vestigial remain of a feeling which sophisticated man should have got rid of, and that the really 'with it' person should be prepared to expose his tastes and peccadilloes before the world for its entertainment and enlightenment.

That view may have some adherents in N.W.1, and it will not be rebuked by E.C.4, but I have no doubt that the overwhelming majority of people agree about privacy. The right to be left alone may not sound a very exciting freedom, but it is the one about which the British people care most . . .

This is the problem. Modern technology has conferred substantial benefits on us. Moreover, it is foolish to regard bits of machinery as though they were human beings and had moral judgments and, therefore, could be labelled good or bad. Nevertheless, we cannot turn away from the fact that modern technology can be and is misused.

I have always said—and this is one of my major concerns in the Bill—that there is no doubt about what is happening in terms of bugging, the use of bugging devices, and the planting of microphones. This has now become the common practice of private detectives and inquiry agents.

I do not know whether hon. Members saw the B.B.C. programme '24 Hours' last night on which a private detective was explaining how very cheap and simple it was to bug a person's home. Another detective produced a suitcase full of these devices. He said that the suitcase was similar to one which every agent carried. I might add that the principal person being interviewed, the first detective, showed a total contempt for the law of trespass. Indeed, he showed a total contempt for the law in general. He admitted that he was a persistent law-breaker and would go on being a persistent law-breaker. He intends to continue to impersonate gas meter inspectors so as to get into people's houses to plant microphones.

This man said that a few prosecutions for trespass would not worry him. He had had them and was prepared to put up with them in future. No doubt he puts it on the bill. He asserts, both publicly and privately, that that attitude to the whole issue is general, if not universal, in his profession, and that his job cannot be accomplished without the use of these devices.

It is all very well for certain professional detective committees to declare such practices unethical. What is the use of that to the citizen? It does not stop it. It does not even control it. Nor does the law control it. It was not devised to control it, anyway. English law did not evolve with a knowledge of devices like these. So it is important to take note of what is occurring, the extent to which it is occurring, and how easy it is for people's privacy to be invaded.

I want to make clear that it is the intrusion that I think is wrong, not the means. I do not want to get the House off on a false trail. It is no worse to bug a person's home than to stand behind the curtains and take down everything that he says, but it is easier. This is what we have to face. Secreting oneself for a few hours behind a curtain is more difficult than whipping into a room and planting a microphone from which a recording can be taken. Therefore, I have every right to claim—and every factor to which we have access proves the claim—that this is not a static practice. It is a persistently growing menace.

I quote again this obligingly frank, if somewhat naive, detective. He said: 'It has mushroomed up in the last few years.' It will mushroom up further, because it is not only private detectives and inquiry agents who use bugs. Newspapers do. They are very shy of talking about it, but they use them.

One national newspaper asked me to see its representative. He was a very nice man. He was very frank and candid. He asked me what would be the position of his paper under the Bill, because it was the common practice of a large national newspaper to send out its reporters with hidden recorders on them so that, under the pretext of having an interview or, for that matter, having a chat, they could record every word that was said.

I want to be absolutely fair. That man did not even understand that that could at least be questionable—not necessarily unlawful, but questionable. It seemed to him to be absolutely in order. Indeed, he felt that the newspaper was being self-denying. It actually put the recorders on the men. It forbore from going around planting them wholesale as part of the normal daily activity of the exposure journalist. He felt that that reflected great credit on his newspaper, and he was a sincere and sensible man . . .

It is not only bugging devices that are causing intrusions. It came to me as a new piece of information to discover that there have already been 5 million pre-employment checks in this country. Of course, there must be checks on a worker being taken on by a firm. It will want to know whether he is competent to do his job. Indeed, the Bill covers such legitimate and valid inquiries. But the real point is that the worker, the individual, has no check on what is going into these pre-employment reports.

When I say that the private detective agencies are one of the greatest sources for collecting such reports, I do not think that the House will be particularly satisfied that the privacy of the individual is likely to be protected by them. There is no check on what is there, and there is no redress if what is there is improper.

I come, now, to deal with civil credit. I think that the credit institutions of this country act with good faith, and a restraint which is absent in other countries, but the fact remains that they instigate the most sweeping and widespread inquiries. Sometimes the mere signing of a hire-purchase form can lead to a detailed inquiry into a person. That is only right and reasonable, and I do not think that the House would ever agree to anything other than that credit companies should have the right to check whether they have potential bad debtors on their hands; of course they should. I have had considerable discussions with credit companies, and I have not met one which has any objection to the Bill. Many of them think that the defence more than covers them in their legitimate activities, but at the moment there is no check of any kind.

I do not think that we should allow in this country the practices which are used by information bureaux in the United States, whereby creditworthiness can include almost anything. It can include nebulous concepts such as marital stability, temperamental affinities, and so on, let alone detailed probes into a person's political views, the practice or non-practice of religion, and so on.

That surely cannot be right. It surely cannot be right to leave a gap in the law, in a society which, all the time, is becoming more and more credit-orientated, for at least the possibility of abuse. Or, to put it another way, there is no possibility of stopping an abuse given the present state of the law, so that again there is an intrusive practice which is growing, and which is dangerous.

53B Eric Heffer (Liverpool, Walton, Labour)
PRIVACY BILL DEBATE

Everyone in the House must be deeply concerned that there has been such a growth of the bugging method, the telephone tapping, and so on. If any hon. Members are not concerned there must be something wrong with them. Whilst the technological revolution is very important, we certainly do not want to build a society such as that described by George Orwell, and the obvious need for all of us is to have privacy.

But there are always problems connected with this question of privacy. Take, for example, dossiers. I can well believe that some hon. Members would be very annoyed if the Press did not have a dossier on them and would want to know why not. I can think of one or two names, but I shall not mention them. So there is another side of the argument. We should remember that public figures are not in precisely the same position as ordinary citizens. A public figure has no right to be a public figure if he is not prepared to be put under a microscope. Our actions are naturally much more liable to be closely examined than the actions of the ordinary citizen. It is quite right that that should be so.

But if we are to have dossiers on public figures, there must, nevertheless, be a limitation on what goes into them. For example, Mr. Alan Watkins, who writes in the *New Statesman*—he writes well, I know him personally and have enjoyed his company—made an important point in that journal on 14th November. He described how two hon. Members—and I do not know who they were—had taken part in a television show and afterwards had some conversation with the television people. A few drinks were going around, there was a free discussion, and the television producer asked them whether they would like to see their dossiers. They said that they would.

They were no doubt delighted that there were dossiers on them. But when they actually saw their dossiers they were deeply concerned because there was much more in them about their private life, as against their public life, which, in my opinion, had no right to be there. Therefore, it is important that we should draw a distinction between the public and the private lies of all individuals. It is vital that we have legislation to deal with these matters . . .

I turn to another aspect and one which has not been discussed very much today—the question not of industrial espionage which, also, has not been discussed very much, although it is important—but another aspect of industrial life with which, as a trade unionist, I have always been concerned. That is the sort of spying interference in the right of the worker that can go on in industry, often unbeknown to him, but sometimes blatantly and openly. That, also, is an intrusion into the privacy of the worker in industry.

For example, there was a construction firm—not the one with which the hon. Member for Folkestone and Hythe (Mr. Costain) is concerned—which felt it necessary to have dossiers on its employees. It wanted to know where the worker had been previously employed, what were his trade union activities, and whether he had ever been a shop steward, and all that sort of thing.

When a joiner or a bricklayer or any other sort of working

man goes for a job I believe that the only matter which the firm has the right to know about is whether he is a fully qualified craftsman and whether he can do his job. If, after a week, under the working rule agreement, the firm finds out that he cannot do his job, it can dismiss him. But trying to find out matters which could be used to stop workers from obtaining jobs because perhaps they were active trade unionists is wrong. It is an invasion of privacy. It may not be one which is discussed very often, but as a former worker in the building industry I felt at that time—and trade unions object strongly as well—that that sort of investigation ought not to take place. We must ensure that it does not.

53C James Callaghan (Cardiff South-East, Labour, Home Secretary) PRIVACY BILL DEBATE

As I rarely sit through a debate on a Friday, I enjoyed this one. We should give ourselves the pleasure of hearing our colleagues more often, except when we intend to make a speech ourselves. Everyone else has enjoyed it and it has been a worth-while debate. Having read and studied this matter, having read the report of 'Justice'—I thank its members for the manner of its production and the study which went into it—and the work of the Society of Labour Lawyers and some of the other publications issued on this matter, having talked it over in my Department, I have come to the conclusion that there is a need for a law of privacy.

This is demonstrable. Certainly, my hon. Friend proved it to me. This is one of the abilities, properly and intelligently used, of back benchers, that they can make Governments think about these problems and, by the intelligent use of parliamentary time, get something done about them.

My hon. Friend has convinced me that we should take some action on this matter. When he asks the second question, however, whether the Bill is the right way to do it, I differ from him. He has not proved it to my satisfaction or, I think, to that of other hon. Members. We will never get unanimity on a matter like this, but we should have more detailed and technical investigation. There is a real difference of approach. One is the lawyers' approach, as I understand the report of 'Justice'.

Although there was some complaint that my hon. Friend the Member for York (Mr. Alexander W. Lyon) made a long speech, it should not be forgotten that he was one of the forerunners in the House in the work in this matter. I pay tribute to him for his work over a period of years, but he thinks—I understand this—that the judges have always been excellent on this question of privacy and that, therefore, if we just lay down the bare outline, we can leave it to them to fill in the content and put flesh on the skeleton.

That is one way of doing it. I accept that, in this field as opposed to others, judges may have a good record. Nevertheless, as he himself said, they have rather opted out of making law in this field. I have, as a parliamentarian, a preference for letting Parliament try to lay down in some detail not only what is the central area of agreement, but also what are the boundaries. Perhaps we cannot do it . . .

There have been many studies of this matter. The courts have dealt satisfactorily with difficult cases arising in these fields of law, but the law on such matters as defamation and trespass is very long-established. Some of the terms in the Bill, like 'substantial' and 'unreasonable', are very imprecise and it might take a number of years for the courts to reach final and authoritative interpretations. In these days the courts are used to having more precise guidance as to the wishes of Parliament. This is the right thing to do and the way in which we should tackle the matter.

My hon. and learned Friend the Member for Derby, North (Mr. MacDermot) said that we should let the Bill go into Committee, but the question is whether this is the right Bill to go into Committee. I do not think that it is. If it is agreed that legislation is needed to give more effective protection to privacy, as I think, will this best be secured by giving individuals the right of redress in the civil courts—some people think that it will be, but I wonder—or will the object of my hon. Friend and other supporters of the Bill be more effectively secured by evoking the sanctions of the criminal law, or it could be a mixture of the two, both the civil and the criminal law?

These are questions that ought to be answered before we embark on legislation. What is more, they are questions of principle which should be decided at Second Reading and not allowed to go to Committee in order to decide major questions of this sort.

The promoters have taken the view, which is a perfectly arguable view, that there should be a civil protection. I am not persuaded of that. But, having taken their stand on the fact that it should be a civil remedy and no more, I am entitled to say to the House that, on balance, the question of alternative remedies, as well as the boundaries of the action to which objection is taken, should be more clearly defined. That cannot be done if at this stage we allow the Bill to go straight into Committee.

When we consider the many diverse areas in which the problem of privacy arises and the extent to which it gives scope for controversy, as has been seen in the debate today, it is by no means self-evident that the right way to solve the problem is through the medium of the Bill as drawn at present, namely, by establishing a right of privacy and providing a civil remedy for its substantial infringement.

I will mention one case which seemed to me to show the inadequacy of the present system and provide a case for a further look at this matter. My attention was drawn to a case of unauthorised telephone tapping and to the fact that the only way in which a prosecution could be taken was under the Theft Act for the theft of electricity. If we can only get at unauthorised telephone tapping by charging whoever did it with the theft of electricity, then there is a case which ought to be looked at much more closely than has happened up to the present.

I wish to make the following proposal to the House and to the promoters of the Bill, who have, in my view, achieved a substantial and signal victory in this matter. The Government, with the agreement of the Lord Chancellor, the Secretary of State for Scotland, and myself, intend to set up a committee on this matter. The terms of reference will be to consider whether legislation is needed to give further protection to the individual citizen and to commercial and industrial interests against intrusions into privacy by private persons or organisations, or by companies, and to make recommendations.

This is not a stalling device. I have already indicated my view that I regard this as a serious matter . . .

SOURCE: *House of Commons Official Report* (23 January 1970)

The Younger Committee was accordingly set up, and its Report *was debated in 1973. Mr Robert Carr was now Home Secretary and spoke first in the debate.*

54A Robert Carr (Mitcham, Conservative, Home Secretary)
DEBATE ON YOUNGER REPORT

There has been considerable concern about the matter of privacy in recent years and it was undoubtedly right to have the whole matter looked into comprehensively in this way. Therefore, perhaps it is worth making a general point about the report which is an encouraging one, namely, that after looking into this matter as it has, the committee did not find a situation which it thought to be very serious or to be one which was fast deteriorating. The committee pointed to several ways in which privacy could be threatened but it has not suggested that a great deal of injury was in fact occurring.

Moreover, it was common ground in the committee that the

existing law provides more effective protection for some kinds of intrusion into privacy than perhaps is generally recognised. It is important that what is available should be drawn to people's attention, because it is often the case that there are remedies which have become forgotten and are generally unknown to people who might benefit from them.

It is probably true that members of the committee differed only in their views of how the acknowledged gap should be filled, and here only on one major issue. A central issue—perhaps the central issue—in the report and the only one on which the committee was divided is the question whether there should be a general legal right of privacy . . .

In considering this question the Government have naturally looked at the experience of other countries. But we feel that the evidence is inconclusive and to some extent distorted by the fact of our different legal tradition. Unlike many other countries, we do not have a written constitution, and the creation of general rights is not the way in which our law has traditionally sought to protect fundamental human freedoms. Freedom of speech, freedom of conscience, the right of free assembly are not in any way guaranteed by statute in this country. But I do not think that the history of our country compared with that of others has shown that these freedoms are less secure for these omissions. Indeed, whether it be because of some peculiar characteristic, some peculiar nature in our people in these islands, or whether it be because of the unusual nature of our constitution—the lack of a written constitution, the lack of a formal statement of these rights—whatever the reasons may be, I think our freedom in these matters is accepted not only by ourselves, but by most other countries as one of the characteristics of Britain.

Moreover, it is not obvious that the citizens of those countries which do have a general right of privacy in their civil codes live in practice in an atmosphere in which privacy is held in more respect than it is here. So the Government believe that the views of the majority of the Younger Committee do carry conviction and should be accepted in on this general and central issue.

I want to emphasise strongly that in accepting the Younger Committee's conclusions on this central point we are not insensitive to the anxiety and annoyance which particular forms of intrusion into privacy can cause. It is simply that we believe, along with the majority of the Younger Committee, that the better approach and an adequate approach is to look for specific measures to deal with particular problems.

One such problem which we want to look at is the harassment and pestering to which people may be subjected, perhaps by the Press or radio or television, for information either on their personal affairs or for other reasons such as sheer curiosity about a celebrity. The Government, therefore, intend to give a further examination to whether the law can or should put some curb on such activities. But in saying that we want to give it further examination, I want to make it absolutely clear that the Government, at this stage at least, are not making a commitment to legislate because it is far from easy to see where and how one could justify the intervention of the criminal law and at what point to draw the line.

Of course, there are some forms of harassment, such as intrusion into private grief, which I think everybody would condemn. But ought it to be unlawful, for example, to mob a pop star who may thrive on such activities, or, for example, to harass, within the law as it now stands, the house agent or the travel agent who has shut up shop after taking his customers' deposits? . . .

The Younger Committee recommended that private detectives should be licensed, with the object of excluding those who were not fit and proper persons. It did not think it practicable to control professional standards or behaviour, and a private detective would get a licence even if he were known to be incompetent. While the Government agree with the object behind this recommendation, we doubt whether the scheme proposed is the best way or an effective way to achieve it. As the committee remarked, the essence of a private detective's work is the invasion of privacy. What it proposes would therefore amount to a positive licence to pry. The public might also inevitably be misled, although the Younger Committee made clear that it was not proposing this sort of protection, into believing that the fact that a person possesses a licence implies some special status, competence or power.

We believe that to be a serious drawback and it is a matter to which chief officers of police attach great importance. The licensing body would have to rely on the police for information about convictions of private detectives, the disclosure of which has itself important privacy implications. We have therefore been considering whether there is an alternative method which would achieve the committee's objectives without the drawbacks and we believe that it means starting the other way round. We have in mind not a scheme of licensing but a scheme of disqualification. A person would be disqualified from acting as a private detective if he had been convicted of an offence involving dishonesty, violence or intrusion into privacy or if he had been given a custodial sentence. It would be essential to ensure that those thereby disqualified were aware of this, for instance by requiring anyone who wished to practise as a private detective to notify the police before starting to act in that capacity so that the police could check.

Mr Alexander W. Lyon (York): Will the Home Secretary tell us what he means when he says that they would be disqualified if convicted of an offence involving intrusion into privacy? What offence would they have committed if we are not to create that offence?

Mr Carr: I think that the hon. Member has bowled me a googly which has penetrated my defences. I think I should not have said 'intrusion of privacy'. I stand corrected by the hon. Gentleman, who is very sharp this morning. It augurs well for his innings later this afternoon.

We believe that in this way we should remove from practice those persons who are not fit and proper to act as detectives

without giving anyone a positive licence which might mislead-
ingly create the impression that a person was positively certified
as being suitable or was specially empowered to make an
inquiry.

Further consultation is needed before we can reach firm
conclusions. I know that the alternative scheme I have outlined needs to be defined in more detail or perhaps, in view of
the hon. Member's intervention, in less detail in some respects.
We have already consulted the chief officers of police, because
they would be closely concerned in the operation of either
scheme. Their general view is that, if there is to be legislation,
disqualification would be preferable to licensing. I should
appreciate hearing hon. Members' views on our proposal . . .

I next deal with computers, a subject in which it is sometimes
difficult to separate myth from reality. The Younger Committee
said that of all the forms of invasion of privacy studied in evidence to it, that involving the use or misuse of computers had
been the least supported in concrete terms. That will perhaps
surprise many people. The committee concluded that 'the
computer as used in the private sector is not at present a threat
to privacy.' Nevertheless it recognised the possibility that such
a threat might become a reality at sometime in the future, and
so it concluded that there was no case for the introduction of
detailed controls, for example the introduction of a registration
or licensing systems, but it made various other recommendations.

The committee suggested, first, the voluntary adoption by
computer users of 10 principles or guidelines which it thought
should apply to the handling of personal information on computers; secondly, that each organisation handling computerised
personal information should examine the idea of appointing a
responsible person to ensure that those principles were observed;
thirdly, that the Government should legislate to provide
machinery in the form of an independent standing commission
to keep developments in this area under review, to receive
complaints about invasions of privacy and, in the light of its

N

findings, to make recommendations for legislative or other safeguards. Finally, it proposed that the Government should, in the light of its report and the concurrent review by officials of the use of computerised personal information stores by Government Departments, consider the possibility of including the public sector within the purview of the proposed standing commission.

The Government propose to publish their conclusions on the subject of computers and privacy in a White Paper later this year. In preparing that White Paper we wish to take account of the views expressed by hon. Members today and in other ways over the next few weeks and the next month or two. The White Paper will include an account of the public reaction to the Younger recommendations and of further inquiries of computer users and experts undertaken on our behalf since the report. The substance of the interdepartmental review of privacy in relation to Government computers will also be included in the White Paper. In preparing the White Paper we shall take account of the Younger Committee's conclusions to which I have just referred, in relation to both private sector and public sector computers, and give our views on the need for further safeguards to protect privacy in both areas.

The White Paper will be a substantial document. It will cover local authorities, the National Health Service and nationalised industries, which were outside the terms of both the Younger Committee and the interdepartmental review. A good deal of consultation and discussion must take place before we can produce the White Paper. Therefore, although I regret it, I ask the House to believe that it is inevitable that it is not yet published and that I cannot today state our conclusions on this important matter.

As there has been a good deal of attention directed at what goes on in Government computers, and as there may be suspicion in some quarters that publication is being held up because we have something to hide, I should like to say that personal information stored on Government computers is at least as

secure as comparable information held on manual systems
previously used by the Government. Methods of computer
security are kept under review. The Younger principles, perhaps better described as a statement of good practice, already
largely underlie the use of computerised personal registers in
Government Departments. But all that will be set out in the
White Paper, which we shall publish as quickly as possible, and
then the House will have to judge and comment on what we say.

54B Shirley Williams (Hitchin, Labour)
DEBATE ON YOUNGER REPORT

I am grateful to the right hon. Gentleman for raising the matter
of the Government's study of the safety of records kept on
computers by the Government. He said that their safety was as
great as that of manual records. But can this view be wholly
shared by the House? In the last three years there has been a
massive computerisation of individual data held on computer
records by the Government. I shall refer to only a few examples.

There has been the setting up of the police computer with its
national recording of criminal offences. There has been the
setting up of data banks by regional hospital boards throughout
the country. The hon. Member for Aylesbury (Mr. Raison)
will be aware that doctors in his area have flatly refused to
co-operate in this matter because they fear that the confidentiality of medical records may be in doubt. There has also been
the setting up of the central vehicle licensing computer at
Swansea and the computerisation of records concerning civil
servants—the so-called prism system. I do not doubt in many
cases the advantages which will flow from more rapid and
better storage of information, but I am profoundly concerned
about some recent developments and I shall mention them
briefly.

Under the Income Tax Management Act 1964 Inland
Revenue records are meant to be revealed only for the purposes
of the duties of Inland Revenue officers, yet we already know

from an answer that the Home Secretary gave to my hon. Friend the Member for Norwood (Mr. John Fraser) that such information is now available for the purposes of tracing illegal immigrants. In his reply the right hon. Gentleman said that this was only with the taxpayer's prior consent. I hope he can assure the House that that is so. I am not clear that that was so in all cases prior to his answer to that Question.

A second instance lies in the use of social service records for various purposes, including the tracing of illegal immigrants and some recent disturbing searches regarding cohabitation by people seeking social service benefits. The wide extension of means testing indicates that we must be more concerned with the confidentiality of social service records than we have been in the past.

A third example, which I have already mentioned, concerns health records. I should like to make it absolutely clear to the House that the linkage of health records between regional hospital boards to create what is, in effect, a nationally-linked system of medical records is being done without any question of the consent of the patients being sought. It needs only a moment's imagination to realise, if one could link up medical records with employment records in such a way as to reveal, for instance, past treatment for psychiatric illnesses or venereal disease, how widely we are extending the power over individuals in a way that frankly I find exceedingly disturbing.

54C Maurice Edelman (Coventry North, Labour) DEBATE ON YOUNGER REPORT

If an investigative or exposure Press goes out of its way to attack an individual or a group of individuals who may not have the capacity, the courage or the endurance to reply to it, then, for precisely the same reason as arises when people are reluctant to go to law when they feel themselves libelled, the Press may be capable of abusing its powers.

I wish to draw attention now to an abuse which took place a few years ago and which has, I believe, proved to be a most sinister development in the history of investigative journalism. I do not wish unduly to argue from the particular to the general, but I must refer to this case because it encapsulates the principle and it has already become the precedent for all sorts of abuse which are taking place to this very day.

I refer to the occasion when *The Times* 'bugged' two policemen who were subsequently convicted on charges of corruption and conspiracy. The House will recall the circumstances. Tape recordings were made of the conversations of the two policemen with a convicted criminal who in turn was acting in collusion with two reporters from *The Times* who had a radio receiver by means of which they were able to record the conversations.

In order to balance that preamble, I should add that on 27th June one of Her Majesty's judges congratulated those journalists on their enterprise. It was reported in *The Times* under the head, 'Judge says two reporters of *The Times* rendered great service in police case'. This is what the learned judge said in the Court of Appeal:

> It is clearly outside our province to make any observations regarding newspaper investigations in general. But, equally clearly, it would be churlish were we to fail to make mention of the great public service rendered by these two reporters.
> It was, it would appear, mainly their intrepidity and skill which laid bare a hideous cancer which, if unchecked, could have done even greater and incalculable damage to law enforcement. It accordingly seems to us only right that we should pay them tribute, and that we do now.

Mr R. C. Mitchell (Southampton, Itchen): Hear, hear.

Mr Edelman: I must say, without disputing the ruling of the learned judge, that I am somewhat surprised that he should have made that *obiter dictum*, and I am surprised also that my hon. Friend should applaud it.

Mr Mitchell: It was very good.

Mr Edelman: I say that because, whatever the guilt subsequently established of the policemen concerned, it was a grave invasion of their rights as citizens, guilty though they proved to be, that *The Times*, in collusion with a convicted criminal, should have set up that apparatus in order to trap two persons in relation to whom, as far as could be told up to that point, nothing had been proved and nothing had been invoked in respect of the police. The appeal judge's tribute to the intrepidity and skill of the journalists opened the doors to investigatory techniques of a most dubious kind.

Mr R. C. Mitchell: Will my hon. Friend suggest how these policemen would have been brought to justice and how the whole case would have been exposed had *The Times* not done what it did?

Mr Edelman: I believe that the function of *The Times* should have been to go to the Commissioner of Police or, failing that, to the Home Secretary to bring such evidence or at least such charges as had been laid to the attention of these people so that they could act. If they had felt compelled to act it would have been appropriate for them to have done so in this way . . .

54D Timothy Raison (Aylesbury, Conservative) DEBATE ON YOUNGER REPORT

What I want to talk about was referred to briefly by the hon. Member for Hitchin (Mrs. Shirley Williams). I am not arguing that abuses are being committed in this respect, but we have an unsatisfactory situation. I am referring to the scheme for hospital activity analysis which was initiated by the Department of Health and Social Security, and in particular to the variation on it operated by the Oxford Regional Hospital Board.

The story goes back to 1969, when the Department issued a circular on the development of hospital activity analysis. I understand that the point was not to build up individual case histories but to build up statistical material from which it would be possible to draw general and no doubt very valuable conclusions, which is a very wise thing. At that stage hospitals were asked to introduce a form and the doctors in my constituency, under the Royal Buckinghamshire and St. John's Hospital Management Committee—although they had not then actually emerged—accepted that.

In 1970 the board notified hospital management committees that it proposed to extend its experimental scheme of record linkage to all hospitals in the Oxford region for the purpose of collecting the data which was already required by the Department. The Department did not ask for identifying details on the form on which the information was to be provided, but the Oxford record linkage study required very full patient identifying details to be included on the form. At that point the doctors in Aylesbury took exception. Later in 1970 the Department introduced a new form which was called HMR 1 Psychiatric. Instructions were given for the form to be completed with full identifying details of every in-patient admitted to mental hospitals. The forms had to be sent to the Department of Health and Social Security at Fleetwood for inclusion in the national psychiatric computer file.

At the same time the Oxford Regional Hospital Board decided to commence the psychiatric information system and asked for the HMR 1 Psychiatric forms to be sent to the DHSS via the board. That would enable the diagnosis and treatment of every psychiatric inpatient in the region to be recorded centrally together with their names and all identifying particulars. In other words, there was a move from a request for material which could be lumped together and used for analytical purposes to a kind of general and very full record of the history of the patients. The details asked for, and asked for particularly of psychiatric patients, included matters which inevitably go very wide—for example, whether the patient had been referred as a result of criminal activities and whether drug-taking came into the patient's history.

There is no doubt that the forms went into enormous detail and gave a full record of things which most hon. Members, assuming that they qualified for them, would be very unhappy

to make public. The medical advisory committee of the Aylesbury hospitals decided that, until Parliament had enacted legal
safeguards to protect the right of patients against wrongful or
unauthorised disclosure of computer medical records, it would
withhold identifying details from record forms sent to the
national psychiatric information service. The Aylesbury doctors
said that they would not send in identifying details.

The reaction of the DHSS was to say that it could not accept
the forms without identifying particulars. After a while it told
the hospital management committee that it had adjusted its
system to allow the Aylesbury forms to be slotted into the
computer without identification. It has confirmed that the
omission of identifying details has not caused any real difficulties to the system although there are certain complications.

I believe that the Aylesbury doctors were absolutely right to
take that stand. They were right because they considered that
it was wrong for them to transmit details about individuals
without the consent or knowledge of those individuals. Secondly,
it is a breach of the notion of medical confidentiality if that kind
of detail can be put on centralised records without stringent
safeguards to prevent such matters being released elsewhere.

I am not saying that there is evidence that information has
come out of the computer which should not have come out.
The Aylesbury doctors are saying that they believe that the
details of the scheme must be made known to the public both to
encourage the discussion which is needed to arrive at the right
solution and to ensure that patients know what is happening.
They say that there should be a form of consent for patients to
sign to indicate whether they are agreeable to specific data
being forwarded for the purpose of medical research and
record-keeping.

Further, the Aylesbury doctors say that the question of data
storage in computers should be placed within a proper legal
framework created by Parliament, which should define individual rights, lay down proper controls and clarify abuses and
penalties. They say that, until there is a system which makes the

position clear, anyone who releases details in an unauthorised way is liable to be subject to penalties with which they may not feel able to co-operate.

54E R. C. Mitchell (Southampton, Itchen, Conservative) DEBATE ON YOUNGER REPORT

Everyone condemns intrusion into private grief by some newspapers. One condemns the taking of photographs, by means of a telescopic lens, of prominent lady politicians sub-bathing in the seclusion of their country estates. Obviously, everyone condemns this sort of thing. Nevertheless, there is a difference between the ordinary person and the public figure. When one decides to become a public figure one gives up in some way a little of one's right to privacy. We as politicians are public figures. We like the Press to print the things which are in our favour. We like them to say what wonderful things we have been saying in the House of Commons, or what wonderful things we have done in our constituencies. We like to use the Press for our own propaganda. We should not be too worried, therefore, if occasionally the Press get hold of a story which is to our disadvantage and print that as well. The public figure who uses the information media for his own purposes should not complain if occasionally he gets one bowled back at him. Those of us in public life have given up some right to privacy which other people may have.

My hon. Friend the Member for Coventry, North (Mr. Edelman) talked about investigatory journalism. I want to refer to one or two cases where, in the last 10 years, but for the Press, people would not have been brought to justice. In April 1963 *The People* exposed the widespread bribery in the football world, and in January 1965 10 footballers were sent to prison for this. In July 1967 the *Daily Mail* exposed Dr. John Petro, who was supplying drugs in London, and in October 1968 Dr. Petro was struck off. In 1969 we had the case of bribery and corruption amongst London detectives, and later two Scotland

Yard detectives were sentenced. In August 1967 the *News of the World* revealed the cruelty to aged patients in State hospitals. The file was handed to the Ministry of Health. In 1969 a committee of inquiry was set up. It found that some patients had been ill-treated at Ely, and the then Secretary of State for Wales announced a tightening up in procedure.

In July 1970 the *News of the World* exposed the abortion racket. In March 1971 a certain doctor who was said to have taken part in the ugly cut-throat competition for his share in the abortion trade was struck off the register. For a time following that, the harassment of and touting for girls at airports almost ceased. In September 1972 the same newspaper exposed property speculators, revealing that developers had bought up semi-derelict houses and, after modernising them with the help of grants, sold them at large profits. In June 1973 local councils were given powers by this House to make profiteers pay back some of those improvement grants. Then there was the exposure in several newspapers of the cruel trade in the export of live animals. In February 1973 the Government banned the export of all live sheep and lambs; and this House last night expressed its views against the wishes of the Government, and I hope the Government will now ban the export of all live animals.

Mr Gorst: I am sure the hon. Gentleman would not want to get the matter out of perspective. He is recounting some of the successes of the Press. Against that, what we never hear about are those occasions when the Press have either hounded or harassed people who have been totally innocent, and this has had nothing to do with the public interest. We never hear about those cases.

Mr Edelman: Before the hon. Gentleman——

Mr Deputy-Speaker (Miss Harvie Anderson): Order. Mr. Mitchell.

Mr Mitchell: That is why I said at the beginning of my remarks that everyone would condemn the sort of behaviour which the hon. Gentleman has mentioned. The tenor of this debate has been fairly critical of the Press, and I thought it only right to put the other side of the picture and to mention some of the successes. I have several other examples which I could quote if necessary. I am convinced that the people concerned would not have been brought to justice, certainly not so quickly, had the Press not investigated and printed these stories and had the Press been afraid of some law.

Mr Edelman: Would my hon. Friend allow me? He has referred to certain observations that I made about the investigatory function of the Press. He has now given a catalogue of the successes which the Press has achieved by exposure journalism. I believe that exposure journalism is a perfectly valid function of the Press, and indeed is desirable. But what I and others criticise is the technique and the means which the Press use in this connection which constitute an abuse and an invasion of privacy.

Mr Mitchell: I observe the distinction made by my hon. Friend. I would not go so far as he does because in some cases the result probably would not have been achieved without using certain techniques to which my hon. Friend objects. One can argue—it is a philosophical question—whether it is better that some people should go free than that these devices should be used, and I think that I should take a slightly different line on that from the one expressed by my hon. Friend the Member for All Saints.

54F Ted Leadbitter (The Hartlepools, Labour) DEBATE ON YOUNGER REPORT

We who talk of our desire to see a fair society, are distressed to find creeping into our nationalised bodies a managerial or arbitrary approach to the affairs with which they are charged which is completely foreign to the hopes and aspirations of those of us who have promoted their existence.

One such debt-collecting agency employed by the gas board wrote to a constituent of mine asking for the payment of certain arrears to the board. It threatened my constituent that, if the money was not paid in a certain time, his name would be given

to its outside van. It threatened that all those offering the
credit facilities which would normally be available to my constituent would be notified and, in effect, my constituent would
be black-listed. Third, it threatened prosecution measures—in
other words, 'We shall take you to court'.

A matter of that kind raises important questions for the
House. In legal terms, what right has a debt-collecting agency
to act on behalf of a nationalised industry? To put it another
way, what right has a nationalised industry to pay public
money to a private firm, which is not licensed in any way, to do
for it what it has the power to do for itself?

If someone owes money to a nationalised industry and the
money is not forthcoming, when capacity to pay exists, a
nationalised industry has the normal procedures available to
take the recalcitrant to court. Why, then, should it employ a
debt-collecting agency? Why should a person be threatened
with public exposure? Why should such a person as my constituent be denied the normal facilities of his fellow men for the
purpose of meeting his family needs?

To be fair, I must say that the gas board, since this case was
brought to its attention, has dispensed with the services of this
debt-collecting agency, but, so it says, only for the time being.
It has also apologised to my constituent because it did not
know that he did not owe it any money. But this raises another
question. The board has much of its business computerised, and
herein lies one of the great problems: would my constituent
have been placed in this position if the proper checks and
balances had been brought into play?

SOURCE: *House of Commons Official Report* (13 July 1973)

A RIGHT OF PRIVACY

*Anyone who is concerned about the manifold threats to privacy which
have been surveyed in this book is bound to ask what safeguards against
them are provided by the law. The answer is far from reassuring. The
Justice Report gave, with the backing of legal knowledge but in*

*straightforward layman's language, a list of situations in which there is
no legal remedy.*

55 Justice Report
NO LEGAL REMEDY

1. You have a secluded garden, overlooked only by a hill
two miles away. One day you are kissing your wife in the
garden when a stranger, standing on a highway on the hill,
takes a photograph of you through a powerful telephoto lens.

2. You and your co-director are in your office, discussing
your company's future marketing strategy. The window is open.
From premises across the street your trade rival, with the
permission of the occupier, records your conversation with a
parabolic microphone.

3. A national credit information bureau makes every reasonable effort to get its information only from the most reliable
sources. The agent whom they employ in your locality has a
grudge against you and knows about some past skeletons in
your cupboard, an accurate version of which he includes in a
report on you which goes on their file. Your credit is ruined.

4. Your employer, unknown to you, has your wife followed
and her friends and neighbours interviewed. The results, with
adverse (but true) comments, go down on your personnel record.

5. You are at home, discussing your business affairs with
your bank manager over the telephone. Where the wires cross a
road, an inquiry agent listens to the whole conversation with an
induction coil. Later, he sells the information to your trade rival.

6. You are a respected member of your local community, but
not in any sense a public figure. One day, your local newspaper
publishes an article about you in which they allude to the facts
that:

(a) twenty-five years ago you were convicted of stealing;
(b) ten years ago, you had an affair with a married woman;
   and
(c) your mother died in a lunatic asylum.

All these statements are true.

7. You have the misfortune to be knocked down by a car driven by a well-known politician and you are badly hurt. With the consent of a member of the hospital staff (but not with that of yourself or your family), a photographer from a news agency takes a picture of you, disfigured and unconscious, in your hospital bed. A magazine to whom he sells it publishes the picture.

8. Your only child, a successful actress, is killed in a car crash. Reporters telephone you night and day, and your house is besieged by photographers from the Press and the television companies, who take pictures of you and your wife whenever you show yourselves at the door. These are published in the national Press and on the television news bulletins.

9. You are the manufacturer of a well-known product and your home telephone number is 'ex-directory.' A popular television personality makes fun of you on his programme, but without being libellous. He screens your private telephone number and suggests that viewers should ring you up. Your telephone does not stop ringing for days: you have to have it disconnected, and lose an important contract as a result.

10. Your brother, who died not long ago, was a homosexual. He was deeply troubled by this, and fought it with almost complete success. Very few people knew about it, but one of them happens to be a friend of your employer (a man of strong prejudices), whom he tells in strict confidence. You are dismissed without being given any reason, and your employer spreads the story far and wide.

In none of these cases would you have any redress as the law now stands, nor would anyone have committed any criminal offence.

SOURCE: *Privacy and the Law, A Report by Justice* (1970)

The Younger Report, quoted earlier but reintroduced here for convenience, meets this criticism in two ways. Firstly, it gives an account of the laws—there are in fact quite a number—which do protect privacy in various contexts. And it cites some recent court cases:

56A Younger Report
LEGAL CONVICTIONS

1. In September 1967 a private detective was convicted at Feltham, Middlesex, of offences against the Wireless Telegraphy Act 1949 for installing a wireless transmitter in a private telephone and using the transmitter without a licence. He was fined £150 and £100 on these counts respectively. He had gained access to the telephone by masquerading as a telephone engineer.

2. In February 1969 two enquiry agents were charged with conspiracy to effect a public mischief in connection with attempts to trace missing debtors by impersonating Inland Revenue officials. Both were found guilty and fined £5000 each: their company was fined £1000. Each was ordered to pay £300 costs and the company £50.

3. In June 1971 two private detectives were convicted at the Old Bailey for (a) conspiring together to contravene the Wireless Telegraphy Act 1949 and (b) conspiracy to trespass, while attempting to obtain evidence for use in a divorce case, by installing and using unlicensed radio transmitters. They were each sentenced to nine months' imprisonment (suspended for three years) and were each fined £300 and ordered to pay £250 costs.

4. In October 1971 a woman private detective and her employer, the proprietor of a private detective agency, were convicted at Lincoln Assizes of conspiring to get confidential information by corrupt means and to offer a bribe in order to obtain 'secret' information from a certain chemical firm. One was fined £100 and the other £1500 on the first charge and each was fined a nominal £1 on the second.

Secondly, the Report made a number of recommendations for new legislation. The most significant of these are:

56B Younger Report
RECOMMENDED LEGISLATION

A major problem with controlling surreptitious surveillance by devices is that, of its nature, it is difficult to detect. Enforcement of a controlling law on this type of activity would therefore be more than usually difficult. For this reason we consider that there should be a new criminal offence of unlawful surveillance by surreptitious means. This should ensure that, where any such act is reasonably suspected, the resources of the police would be available to investigate and prosecute it.

The criminal offence of surreptitious surveillance by means of a technical device would comprise the following elements:

a. a technical device;

b. surreptitious use of the device;

c. a person who is, or his possessions which are, the object of surveillance;

d. a set of circumstances in which, were it not for the use of the device, that person would be justified in believing that he had protected himself or his possessions from surveillance whether by overhearing or observation;

e. an intention by the user to render those circumstances ineffective as protection against overhearing or observation; and

f. absence of consent by the victim.

. . . We . . . recommend that the Government should legislate to provide itself with machinery for keeping under review the growth in and techniques of gathering personal information and processing it with the help of computers. Such machinery should take the form of an independent body with members drawn from both the computer world and outside. For the sake of convenience we call it here a standing commission and it may be helpful if we say something about what we think it ought to do.

We envisage that it should collect information about computerised personal information stores: their prevalence, purpose, detail, linkage, commercial use and management. It should review the principles of handling personal information laid down in this chapter to determine their relevance and adequacy in a changing situation and consider the case for giving them legislative force. It could receive complaints about invasions of privacy by the users of computerised information stores. In the light of its findings it should, from time to time, make recommendations as it saw fit for legislative or other controls for safeguarding the handling of personal information in computerised stores.

SOURCE: *Report of the Committee on Privacy* (1972)

However, there is a body of opinion which holds that the law should provide a general right of privacy, and create a general offence of intrusion into privacy, as distinct from piecemeal legislation in specific contexts. The classic case for a right of privacy was set out in 1890 in an article by two American lawyers, Louis D. Brandeis (later a distinguished Justice of the Supreme Court) and his partner Samuel D. Warren. Warren and Mrs. Warren had been prominent in Boston society and had been annoyed by receiving unwelcome publicity in the press.

57A Brandeis and Warren
THE CASE FOR A RIGHT TO PRIVACY

That the individual shall have full protection in person and in property is a principle as old as the common law; but it has been found necessary from time to time to define anew the exact nature and extent of such protection. Political, social, and economic changes entail the recognition of new rights, and the common law, in its eternal youth, grows to meet the demands of society. Thus, in very early times, the law gave a remedy only for *physical* interference with life and property. Then the 'right to life' served only to protect the subject from battery in its

o

various forms; liberty meant freedom from actual restraint; and the right to property secured to the individual his lands and his cattle. Later there came a recognition of man's spiritual nature, of his feelings and his intellect. Gradually the scope of these legal rights broadened; and now the right to life has come to mean the right to enjoy life,—the right to be let alone; the right to liberty secures the exercise of extensive civil privileges; and the term 'property' has grown to comprise every form of possession—intangible, as well as tangible.

Thus, with the recognition of the legal value of sensations, the protection against actual bodily injury was extended to prohibit mere *attempts* to do such injury; that is, the putting another in fear of such injury. From the action of battery grew that of assault. Much later there came a qualified protection of the individual against offensive noises and odors, against dust and smoke, and excessive vibration. The law of nuisance was developed. So regard for human emotions soon extended the scope of personal immunity beyond the body of the individual. His reputation, the standing among his fellow-men, was considered, and the law of slander and libel arose. Man's family relations became a part of the legal conception of his life, and the alienation of a wife's affections was held remediable. Occasionally, the law halted—as in its refusal to recognise the intrusion by seduction upon the honor of the family. But even here the demands of society were met. A mean fictional remedy— the loss of services—was ordinarily afforded. Similar to the expansion of the right to life was the growth of the legal conception of property. From corporeal property arose the incorporeal rights issuing out of it; and then there opened the wide realm of intangible property, in the products and processes of the mind, as works of literature and art, goodwill, trade secrets, and trademarks.

This development of the law was inevitable. The intense intellectual and emotional life, and the heightening of sensations which came with the advance of civilisation, made it clear to one that only a part of the pain, pleasure, and profit of life lay in physical things. Thoughts, emotions, and sensations demanded legal recognition, and the beautiful capacity for growth which characterises the common law enabled the judges to afford the requisite protection, without the interposition of the legislature . . .

Of the desirability—indeed of the necessity—of some such protection, there can, it is believed, be no doubt. The press is overstepping in every direction the obvious bounds of propriety and of decency. Gossip is no longer the resource of the idle and of the vicious, but has become a trade, which is pursued with industry as well as effrontery. To satisfy a prurient taste the details of sexual relations are spread broadcast in the columns of the daily papers. To occupy the indolent, column upon column is filled with idle gossip, which can only be procured by intrusion upon the domestic circle. The intensity and complexity of life, attendant upon advancing civilisation, have rendered necessary some retreat from the world, and man, under the refining influence of culture, has become more sensitive to publicity, so that solitude and privacy have become more essential to the individual; but modern enterprise and invention have, through invasions upon his privacy, subjected him to mental pain and distress, far greater than could be inflicted by mere bodily injury.

Brandeis and Warren went on to deal with the argument that the law of defamation (or libel) was sufficient to protect privacy.

57B Brandeis and Warren
LAW OF DEFAMATION

The principle on which the law of defamation rests covers, however, a radically different class of effects from those for which attention is now asked. It deals only with damage to reputation, with the injury done to the individual in his external relations to the community, by lowering him in the estimation of his fellows. The matter published of him, however widely circulated, and however unsuited to publicity, must, in order to be actionable, have a direct tendency to injure him in his intercourse with others, and even if in writing or in print, must subject him to the hatred, ridicule, or contempt of his fellowmen— the effect of publication upon his estimate of himself and upon his own feelings not forming an essential element in the cause of action. In short, the wrongs and correlative rights recognised by the law of slander and libel are in their nature material rather than spiritual. That branch of the law simply extends the protection surrounding physical property to certain of the conditions necessary or helpful to worldly prosperity. On the other hand, our law recognises no principle by which compensation can be granted for mere injury to the feelings. However painful the mental effects upon another of an act, though purely wanton or even malicious, yet if the act itself is otherwise lawful, the suffering inflicted is without legal remedy. Injury of feelings may indeed be taken account of in ascertaining the amount of damages when attending what is recognised as a legal injury; but our system, unlike the Roman law, does not afford a remedy even for mental suffering which results from mere contumely and insult, from an intentional and unwarranted violation of the 'honor' of another . . .

These considerations lead to the conclusion that the protection afforded to thoughts, sentiments, and emotions expressed through the medium of writing or of the arts, so far as it consists in preventing publication, is merely an instance of the enforcement of the more general right of the individual to be let alone. It is like the right not to be assaulted or beaten, the right not to be imprisoned, the right not to be maliciously prosecuted, the right not to be defamed. In each of these rights, as indeed in all other rights recognised by the law, there inheres the quality of being owned or possessed—and (as that is the distinguishing attribute of property) there may be some propriety in speaking of those rights as property. But, obviously, they bear little resemblance to what is ordinarily comprehended upon that term. The principle which protects personal writings and all other personal productions, not against theft and physical appropriation, but against publication in any form, is in reality not the principle of private property, but that of an inviolate personality.

If we are correct in this conclusion, the existing law affords a principle which may be invoked to protect the privacy of the individual from invasion either by the too enterprising press, the photographer, or the possessor of any other modern device for recording or reproducing scenes or sounds. For the protection afforded is not confined by the authorities to those cases where any particular medium or form of expression has been adopted, nor to products of the intellect. The same protection is afforded to emotions and sensations expressed in a musical composition or other work of art as to a literary composition; and words spoken, a pantomime acted, a sonata performed, is no less entitled to protection than if each had been reduced to writing. The circumstances that a thought or emotion has been recorded in a permanent form renders its identification easier, and hence may be important from the point of view of evidence, but it has no significance as a matter of substantive right. If, then, the decisions indicate a general right to privacy for thoughts, emotions, and sensations, these should receive the same protection, whether expressed in writing, or in conduct, in conversation, in attitudes, or in facial expression.

It may be urged that a distinction should be taken between the deliberate expression of thoughts and emotions in literary or artistic compositions and the casual and often involuntary expression given to them in the ordinary conduct of life. In other words, it may be contended that the protection afforded is granted to the conscious products of labor, perhaps as an encouragement to effort. This contention, however plausible, has, in fact, little to recommend it. If the amount of labor involved be adopted as the test, we might well find that the effort to conduct one's self properly in business and in domestic relations had been far greater than that involved in painting a picture or writing a book; one would find that it was far easier to express lofty sentiments in a diary than in the conduct of a noble life. If the test of deliberateness of the act be adopted, much casual correspondence which is now accorded full protection would be excluded from the beneficent operation of existing rules. After the decisions denying the distinction attempted to be made between those literary productions which it was intended to publish and those which it was not, all considerations of the amount of labor involved, the degree of deliberation, the value of the product, and the intention of publishing must be abandoned, and no basis is discerned upon which the right to restrain publication and reproduction of such so-called literary and artistic works can be rested, except the right to privacy, as a part of the more general right to the immunity of the person,—the right to one's personality.

SOURCE: Louis D. Brandeis and Samuel D. Warren. 'The Right to Privacy', *Harvard Law Review* (15 December 1890). The full text is reprinted in Morris L. Ernst and Alan U. Schwarz. *Privacy* (1968)

As I noted in the Introduction, three attempts have been made to create a general right of privacy in British law. The following is the text of Mr Brian Walden's Bill:

58 Brian Walden MP
PRIVACY BILL

A Bill to

Establish a right of privacy, to make consequential amendments to the law of evidence, and for connected purposes.

BE IT ENACTED by the Queen's most Excellent Majesty, by and with the advice and consent of the Lords Spiritual and Temporal, and Commons, in this present Parliament assembled, and by the authority of the same, as follows:—

Right of action for infringement of privacy

1. Any substantial and unreasonable infringement of a right of privacy taking place after the coming into force of this Act shall be actionable at the suit of any person whose right of privacy has been so infringed.

Joinder of parties

2. In any such action the plaintiff may join as a defendant any person who—

(*a*) has committed the infringement; or

(*b*) has knowingly been party to the infringement; or

(*c*) knowing of the infringement, has made any use thereof for his own benefit or to the detriment of the plaintiff.

Defences

3. In any such action it shall be a defence for any defendant to show that—

(*a*) the defendant, having exercised all reasonable care, neither knew nor intended that his conduct would constitute an infringement of the right of privacy of any person; or

(*b*) the plaintiff, expressly or by implication, consented to the infringement; or

(*c*) where the infringement was constituted by the publication of any words or visual images, there were reasonable grounds for the belief that such publication was in the public interest; or

(*d*) the defendant's acts were reasonable and necessary for the protection of the person, property or lawful business or other interests of himself or of any other person for whose benefit or on whose instructions he committed the infringement; or

(*e*) the infringement took place in circumstances such that, had the action been one for defamation, there would have been available to the defendant a defence of absolute or qualified privilege, provided that if the infringement was constituted by a publication in a newspaper, periodical or book, or in a sound or television broadcast, any defence under this paragraph shall be available only if the defendant also shows that the matters published were of public concern and their publication was for the public benefit; or

(*f*) the defendant acted under authority conferred upon him by statute or by any other rule of law.

Remedies

4.—(1) In any such action the court may—

(*a*) award damages;

(*b*) grant an injunction if it shall appear just and convenient;

(*c*) order the defendant to account to the plaintiff for any profits which he has made by reason or in consequence of the infringement;

(*d*) order the defendant to deliver up to the plaintiff all articles or documents which have come into his possession by reason or in consequence of the infringement.

(2) In awarding damages the court shall have regard to all the circumstances of the case, including—

(*a*) the effect on the health, welfare, social, business or financial position of the plaintiff or his family;

(*b*) any distress, annoyance or embarrassment suffered by the plaintiff or his family; and

(*c*) the conduct of the plaintiff and the defendant both before and after the infringement, including any apology or offer of amends made by the defendant or anything done by the defendant to mitigate the consequences of the infringement for the plaintiff.

Limitation

5. No such action shall be brought more than three years

from the time when the plaintiff first became aware, or by the use of reasonable diligence could have become aware, of the infringement, nor in any case more than six years after the cause of action accrued to the plaintiff.

Miscellaneous provisions

6. The right of action conferred by this Act shall be in addition to and not in derogation of any right of action or other remedy available otherwise than by virtue of this Act, provided that this section shall not be construed as requiring any damages awarded in an action brought by virtue of this Act to be disregarded in assessing damages in any proceedings instituted otherwise than by virtue of this Act and arising out of the same transaction.

Rules of court

7. The Lord Chancellor may make rules regulating the procedure of the court for the trial of actions for the infringement of the right of privacy and may by those rules make provision:

(a) where the action has been begun in or transferred to the High Court, for trial by judge and jury upon the application of any party to the action;

(b) for the trial of the action or of any interlocutory proceedings therein or any appeal therefrom otherwise than in open court.

Amendment of law of evidence

8. From and after the coming into force of this Act no evidence obtained by virtue or in consequence of the actionable infringement of any right of privacy by any of the means described in paragraphs (a), (b), (c) or (d) of section 9 (1) of this Act shall be admissible in any civil proceedings.

Definitions

9.—(1) 'Right of privacy' means the right of any person to be protected from intrusion upon himself, his home, his family, his relationships and communications with others, his property and his business affairs, including intrusion by—

(a) spying, prying, watching or besetting;

(b) the unauthorised overhearing or recording of spoken words;

(c) the unauthorised making of visual images;

(d) the unauthorised reading or copying of documents;

(e) the unauthorised use or disclosure of confidential information, or of facts (including his name, identity or likeness) calculated to cause him distress, annoyance or embarrassment, or to place him in a false light;

(f) the unauthorised appropriation of his name, identity or likeness for another's gain.

(2) 'Family' means husband, wife, child, step-child, parent, step-parent, brother, sister, half-brother, half-sister, step-brother, step-sister (in each case whether legitimate or illegitimate and whether living or dead).

(3) 'The court' means the High Court or any county court.

Amendment of Administration of Justice Act 1960 (1960 c. 65)

10. In section 12 (1) of the Administration of Justice Act 1960 (which relates to the publication of information relating to proceedings in private) there shall be inserted immediately after paragraph (d) the following new paragraph—

'(dd) where the court sits in private pursuant to rules of court made under the power conferred by section 7 of the Right of Privacy Act 1970.'

Application to Crown, citation and commencement

11.—(1) This Act shall bind the Crown.

(2) This Act may be cited as the Right of Privacy Act 1970.

(3) This Act shall come into force on 1st January 1971.

SOURCE: Appendix to *Report of the Committee on Privacy* (1972)

Fourteen members of the Younger Committee rejected the idea of such legislation; only two were in favour of it. We may suitably conclude our survey of the privacy problem by setting out the arguments on each side— in the Report itself, and in a minority report written by Mr Alexander Lyon, MP. The majority view was expressed in these terms:

59A Younger Report
COMMITTEE'S CONCLUSIONS ON LEGISLATION

Any general civil remedy would require hardly less general qualification in order to enable the courts (the judge or judge and jury) to achieve an acceptable balance between values implicit in respect for privacy and other values of at least equal importance to the well-being of society. We have particularly in mind the importance in a free society of the unimpeded circulation of true information and the occasions which would inevitably arise, if there were a general civil remedy for the protection of privacy, in which the courts would be called upon to balance, by reference to the 'public interest', society's interest in the circulation of truth against the individual's claim for privacy.

We appreciate that there are countries (of which we give examples in Appendix J) in which it is precisely this balancing function which is left to the courts; and we point out in Appendix I that in English law the protection which is given to privacy by the action for breach of confidence may involve the courts in deciding whether the remedy should be refused on the grounds that the disclosure in question (as, for example, when it relates to the commission of a crime) was in the public interest. The vital difference, however, between decisions on what is in the public interest, taken by the courts in countries where a general remedy for invasions of privacy exists, and the decisions on the public interest taken by English courts in cases under existing laws which are relevant to the protection of specific aspects of privacy, is that the judicial function in the latter is much more circumscribed. Thus, in an action for breach of confidence the court is faced initially with a disclosure of information which has been given in confidence; similarly, in an action for defamation no question of the public interest arises until there is before the court a defamatory statement which is untrue. It is clear that the function of the courts in such circumstances is a less difficult one and one which is likely to give rise to less controversy than that which would face a court which was called upon to apply a much more general law to cases in which no relationship of confidence existed and no false statement had been made. In such cases a court would in effect have to make an unguided choice, in the light of the public interest, between values which, in the abstract, might appear to have equal weight. We recognise that the courts could be given the task of considering, in the factual context of each case, whether a general right to privacy should be upheld against the claims of other values, in particular the value of the free circulation of true information. But we think that such a task might first make the law uncertain, at least for some time until the necessary range of precedents covering a wide range of situations had been established; and it might secondly extend the judicial role, as it is generally understood in our society, too far into the determination of controversial questions of a social and political character . . .

Looking at the field as a whole, we have expressed the view that the existing law provides more effective relief from some kinds of intrusion into privacy than is generally appreciated. In particular it is our opinion that the law on breach of confidence, if some of its present ambiguities were to be authoritatively clarified (if necessary by legislation), would turn out to be a practical instrument for dealing with many complaints in the privacy field.

We have already referred to the need to balance the right of privacy against other and countervailing rights, in particular freedom of information and the right to tell the truth freely unless compelling reasons for a legal limitation of this right can be adduced. We have often found this balance difficult to strike. At every stage we have been conscious of differing judgments about the precise area of privacy which should be protected under each heading and about the considerations of 'public interest' which might be held in each case to justify intrusion and so to override the right of privacy. These uncertainties are, no doubt, largely the consequence of the acknowledged lack of any clear and generally agreed definition of what privacy itself is; and of the only slightly less intractable problem of deciding precisely what is 'in the public interest' or, in a wider formulation, 'of public interest' . . .

A number of other countries in Europe, America and the Commonwealth, have adopted legislation in wide and general terms. While the effectiveness of these laws varies from country to country, there is evidence that some practical use is made of them and no evidence that the information media have complained that these laws unduly restrict their legitimate activities. It seems a natural deduction from this that similar action could usefully be undertaken in the United Kingdom without risk. We have naturally paid close attention to the experience of other countries, but we have noted that the methods of adjusting domestic legislation to the requirements of international agreements differ widely from one signatory state to another, and that this has been markedly true in the field of human rights. This is firstly because some legal systems are readier than others to declare a general right and then to leave to the courts the development of effective sanctions against violations of the right. The second relevant consideration is the difference in the extent to which existing laws in particular countries are already believed to provide sufficiently for the protection of the new right. With regard to the first point we think that the best way to ensure regard for privacy is to provide specific and effective sanctions against clearly defined activities which unreasonably frustrate the individual in his search of privacy. As far as the second point is concerned, we have already described in detail the considerable extent to which privacy is already protected by existing English law. We have noted that in some countries, where the law of defamation is less developed than in England, new laws for the protection of privacy are being used in cases which in England would fall squarely under the heading of defamation. In Germany, we were told, the dividing line between privacy and defamation is already blurred. We do not ourselves favour a similar development here, believing that the law should continue to distinguish clearly in the sanctions which it provides between statements which are both defamatory and untrue and statements which, even if they may be offensive on other grounds, are neither of these things.

This raises the question whether the method which we have adopted is nevertheless inadequate because it leaves the citizen without a legal remedy for important kinds of intrusion upon his privacy; and whether a general right of privacy, which would fill in these gaps, would in practice carry with it serious dangers to the legitimate circulation of information, which is an important value in any democratic society. We have concluded that, so far as the principal areas of complaint are concerned, and especially those which arise from new technological developments, our specific recommendations are likely to be much more effective than any general declaration. Having covered these areas, we do not think that what remains uncovered is extensive; and our evidence does not suggest that the position in the uncovered area is deteriorating. We think moreover that to cover it by a blanket declaration of a right of privacy would introduce uncertainties into the law, the repercussions of which upon free circulation of information are difficult to foresee in detail but could be substantial.

We have found privacy to be a concept which means widely different things to different people and changes significantly over relatively short periods. In considering how the courts could handle so ill-defined and unstable a concept, we conclude that privacy is ill-suited to be the subject of a long process of definition through the building up of precedents over the years, since the judgments of the past would be an unreliable guide to any current evaluation of privacy. If, on the other hand, no body of judge-made precedent were built up, the law would remain, as it would certainly have to begin, highly uncertain and subject to the unguided judgments of juries from time to time. It is difficult to find any firm evidential base on which to assess the danger to the free circulation of information which might result from a legal situation of this kind. The press and broadcasting authorities have naturally expressed to us their concern about any extension into the field of truthful publication of the sort of restraints at present imposed on them by the law of defamation, especially if the practical limits of the extension are bound to remain somewhat indeterminable for a period of years. We do not think these fears can be discounted and we do not forget that others besides the mass media, for instance biographers, novelists or playwrights, might also be affected. We already have some experience of the uncertainties which result, for instance in obscenity cases, when courts of law are asked to make judgments on controversial matters, where statutory definitions are unsatisfactory, and social and moral opinion fluctuates rapidly.

It would, in our view, be unwise to extend this kind of uncertainty into a new branch of the law, unless there were compelling evidence of a substantial wrong, which must be righted even at some risk to other important values. Within the area covered by our terms of reference, evidence of this kind has been conspicuously lacking and we therefore see no reason to recommend that this risk should be taken.

Finally, we repeat what we said at the outset of this chapter. Privacy, however defined, embodies values which are essential to a free society. It requires the support of society as a whole. But the law is only one of the factors determining the climate of a democratic society and it is often only a minor factor. Education, professional standards and the free interplay of ideas and discussion through the mass media and the organs of political democracy can do at least as much as the law to establish and maintain standards of behaviour. We have explained in this report that we see risks in placing excessive reliance on the law in order to protect privacy. We believe that in our recommendations we have given to the law its due place in the protection of privacy and we see no need to extend it further.

Mr Lyon replied:

59B Alexander Lyon MP
MINORITY REPORT ON LEGISLATION

Though the scale of the problem may be small the consequences for the person affected may be catastrophic. The revelation of an industrial secret, financial difficulty, a domestic tragedy or a sexual deviation may cause irreparable damage to the individual and his family. Even the fact that what he thought was private is known to others may create a sense of outrage though the information is not damaging in itself. Lord Goodman in his evidence on behalf of the Newspapers Proprietors Association suggested that privacy was just about sex and now that we were more broad minded the problem was diminishing. That showed lamentable misjudgment.

It is because the damage to the individual may be so great that I think it wrong to leave him without a remedy. A general tort would meet most of the cases, but before I turn to its merits, I consider the criticisms of my colleagues.

... The most cogent criticism was that a general law would inhibit the dissemination of truth. No one doubts the importance to be attached to truth in a civilised society. I welcome the present trend to a more open discussion of public issues based on full disclosure of the facts. But that is far from saying that the public is entitled to know *all* the truth about an individual or group. Some area of a man's life is his business alone. The Orwellian nightmare of '1984' was unpalatable not only for 'Newspeak' but for the complete absence of escape from the regime. I found the lack of privacy more disturbing than the distortion of truth.

My colleagues recognise that a balance has to be kept between the public's right to know and the individual's right to a
private life. They claim that a general law would be an unjustifiable suppression of the truth. The law already puts curbs
on dissemination of true facts in the area of breach of confidence,
criminal libel, copyright and patent. To these we now propose
to add curtailment of the use of electronic and photographic
devices and the use of information obtained by unlawful
methods.

In addition they support stronger curbs on the dissemination
of truth which depend on voluntary action. The journalist and
the banks are to be goaded into improving their standards.
This acknowledges that we all have a moral obligation to re-
frain from passing on truthful facts where they would be hurtful
and no useful purpose would be served.

In other words truth is not inviolate, any more than any
other value in our society. When it conflicts with the commend-
able interest of privacy who must draw the line? At present it
is the intruder himself. I think that in those cases where an
individual can be seriously damaged by a wrong judgment of
the intruder, he ought to have the right to ask society at large
to adjudicate. The only acceptable instrument we have devised
is the law.

Confounded on general principle, the detractors of a general
right take refuge in prophecies of doom. The new tort, they
say, would lead to a spate of blackmailing actions. The majority
candidly admit that this has not been the experience of France,
Germany, Canada, the USA or any other country where
general rights have been created. Resort to law is expensive and
dissuades most potential litigants. The press cite defamation as
an area where unmeritorious cases succeed, but this is frequently because accident is no defence to defamation whereas
all the suggested drafts of a tort of privacy have required a
deliberate intention to intrude. Both experience and principle
suggest that the number of cases under such legislation would
be small.

P

Nevertheless, the critics continue, the threat of legal action may cause those whose duty is to reveal the truth for the public good to limit their activities. If that means that unjustifiable intrusions into individual privacy are controlled, the public in my view will benefit. All justifiable intrusions could be protected by the defences which would be written into any legislation.

If there are some disadvantages to the general right and the number of people assisted will be small is it necessary to legislate? The same argument might have been used in relation to the legal remedies of trespass, nuisance and even negligence. Relatively few people use these remedies each year but they are considered essential parts of the law. They raise similar issues of a balance of conflicting interests and some imprecision of definition. Because the individual would feel a sense of outrage if he was injured in these ways without legal redress, society has thought it right to give legal protection. In a number of western countries similar general protection has been given for privacy without any of the consequences alleged by the critics. It is significant that when the Committee felt offended by new devices for surveillance, it decided to legislate, even though there were no serious complaints from the public . . .

Advantages of the general tort

First, it would cover almost all the privacy situations which could be conceived, even those which have not yet become apparent. If we had legislated on privacy before the war we would not have included electronic devices. Parliamentary time is restricted and every new advance demands a long and sometimes exhausting campaign. It is much better to set out the principles on which the courts can act and leave them to develop the law as need requires. Most of our common law was created in this way and, provided the principles are clear, the courts are well able to undertake the task.

Some criticism of this approach betrayed a suspicion of the conservatism of the judges. British judges are not at their best in developing social policy. Our tradition in this respect differs from the Americans where lawyers commonly discuss issues of wages, social benefits and education. In England these matters are left to Parliament or to administrative tribunals outside the courts. But the problem of privacy is one of balancing conflicting freedoms, which raises issues well understood by British judges and they already have some experience in matters relating to privacy.

Second, it gives a remedy to all those seriously prejudiced by intrusions into privacy. As the Committee considered specific remedies for each privacy situation, we frequently rejected proposals for legislation as too cumbersome for the complaints disclosed. Thus the major portion of credit checking in this country is carried out by two responsible firms against whom there was no complaint. It seemed too onerous to create new statutory controls to deal with any smaller firms who might not adopt the same standards. But anyone injured by the activities of such a firm would have a redress if there was a general tort.

Third, it gives teeth to many of our other recommendations. If a computer operator knew that his activities might lead to a suit for damages, he would be more likely to respond to the code of principles we enunciate.

Fourth, it allows juries to set the standards in a constantly changing area of human values. If private enquiry agents are to lose their certificates of registration for unreasonable intrusion into privacy, who is to decide what is reasonable? The Home Office? The police? I would prefer a jury as more representative of public opinion.

Fifth, it would provide an effective remedy for any unreasonable behaviour. Not only would damages reimburse financial loss or mollify injured feelings, but an injunction would be a useful deterrent to prevent anticipated intrusions into privacy. These remedies would make potential intruders consider carefully before acting and would, in itself, reduce the number of bad cases. No worthy exhortation to better behaviour is likely to be so effective.

Sixth, no general remedy is likely to gain Parliamentary approval if it did not include government activities. The result of my colleagues' recommendations is that the government has succeeded in keeping its activities to itself although many would agree that government intrusion is potentially more dangerous and annoying. A general tort would easily have been amended to cover all those government activities which were not authorised by law. This in turn would have lent support to those who are critical of government's existing powers to intrude.

SOURCE: *Report of the Committee on Privacy* (1972)

Suggestions for Further Reading

The most comprehensive books on privacy are American and give information primarily on conditions in the United States; they are, however, important reading because of the general implications. Among such books (all available in Britain) are:

ERNST, MORRIS L. and SCHWARZ, ALAN U. *Privacy* (1968)

LONG, SENATOR EDWARD V. *The Intruders* (New York, 1967)

MILLER, ARTHUR R. *The Assault on Privacy* (1971)

WESTIN, ALAN F. *Privacy and Freedom* (1970)

Miller provides references to hearings before Committees of the US Senate and House of Representatives. Miller and Westin have large bibliographies with references to articles as well as books.

A great deal of information from all over the world is contained in two United Nations documents: *Report of the Secretary-General on Human Rights and Scientific and Technological Development to the Commission on Human Rights* (E/CN4/1028, 1970); and another *Report* with the same title (E/CN4/1116, 1973). These can be borrowed in mimeographed form from the UN Information Office in London.

Books and pamphlets on specifically British conditions include:

Computers and Freedom (Conservative Research Department, 1968)

HMSO. *Report of the Committee on Privacy* (1972)

JUSTICE. *Privacy and the Law* (Report by a Justice committee, 1970)

MADGWICK, DONALD. *Privacy under Attack* (National Council for Civil Liberties, 1968)

PAYNE, RONALD. *Private Spies* (1967)

ROWE, B. C. (ed). *Privacy, Computers and You* (National Computing Centre, 1972)

RULE, JAMES B. *Private Lives and Public Surveillance* (1973)

WARNER, MALCOLM and STONE, MICHAEL. *The Data Bank Society* (1970)

Acknowledgements

Grateful acknowledgements are due to the following for permission to reprint material:

The Bodley Head Ltd and Atheneum Publishers Inc for extracts from *Privacy and Freedom*, by Alan F. Westin.

The Child Poverty Action Group for extracts from *As Man and Wife?* by Ruth Lister.

The Guardian for extracts from various articles.

Her Majesty's Stationery Office for extracts from the *Report of the Committee on Privacy*.

Justice for extracts from its report, *Privacy and the Law*.

Allen Lane, Penguin Press Ltd and Schocken Books Inc for extracts from *Private Lives and Public Surveillance*, by James B. Rule.

MacGibbon & Kee Ltd for extracts from *Privacy*, by Morris L. Ernst and Alan U. Schwarz.

The National Council for Civil Liberties for extracts from *Privacy under Attack*, by Donald Madgwick, and from NCCL evidence to the Committee on Privacy.

Penguin Books Ltd for extracts from *Warwick University Limited*, edited by E. P. Thompson.

University of Michigan Press for extracts from *The Assault on Privacy*, by Arthur R. Miller.

Index

ABD Organisation, 135
Access cards, 149
Ace Detective Agency, 136
'A' Code on cohabitation, 110–11
Administration of Justice Act (1970), 159
Applications for employment, questionnaires for, 160–1
Aptitude tests, 41–4, 44–6, 47–8
Arrest, police powers of, 90
Assessments, *see* Psychological tests; Reactive assessment
Association of British Investigators, 141–2, 144
Association of British Private Detectives, 141–2
'AX' Code on cohabitation, 110–11

Bankers' references, 146–9
Banking organisations, 145–9
Bankruptcies, 152
Barclaycards, 149
Bardot, Brigitte, 126–8
Baxter, Sydney L., 171
BBC, 132
BDS, *see* British Debt Services
Beck, Stanley M., 33–4
Black, Miss (cohabitation case), 114–15
Blacklisting, 156, 196
Blackmail, 140
Brandeis, Louis D., 201–6
Brave New World (A. Huxley), 19
Brett, Mrs (cohabitation case), 120–1
British Computer Society, 81–2
British Debt Services, 150–4
Brown, Mrs (cohabitation case), 113–14
Bugging devices: described, 31, 32–3; police use of, 37–8; where purchasable, 38–40; 135, 173 (mentioned)
Butterworth, Dr J. B., 167
Buttons, radio devices disguised as, 30

Callaghan, James (MP), 178–81
Cambridge University Appointments Board, 164–5
Cameras, use of, 28–30
Campaign for the Limitation of Secret Police Powers (CLSPP), 96–105
Capital Bureau of Investigations, 136
Carr, Robert (MP), 181

225

Cash registers linked to computers, 64
Catchpole, N. P., 167
Child Poverty Action Group, 110, 118–19
Citizens' Rights Office, 112, 119
Clarke, G. F., 99–100
Clother, John, 102
CLSPP, see Campaign for the Limitation of Secret Police Powers
Coates, Dr John, 166
Code numbers for computers, dangers of, 64
Cohabitation, 108–21
Committee of London Clearing Banks, 145, 148
Committee on Privacy, see Privacy, Committee on
Computers, 19, 52–83 passim: damaging or distorted information from, 65–7; how used in USA, 53–6; information fed to, access to, 63–5; master files for every person, 53–6; mistakes by, 74–5; multi-access to, 63; obsolescence of cash and, 54, 59–60; quantity of in UK, 57–8; range of information possible in, 58–60; recommendations for privacy in, 78–81; reliability of, 81–2; safeguards for privacy in, 75–6, 77, 185, 187, 188; storage of medical histories in, 71–4; storage of psychiatric data in, 68–71; used for police records, 93–4, 187 (see also Police Records); use of 'real time' in, 63
Condon, Judith, 168–9
Consumers' Association, 147–8

Control of Information Bill, 155–6
Cooke, Maureen, 107
Cooley, Mr Justice, 12
Coombes, Keva, 166
Corkery, Michael, 140
Court cases, publicity of, 131
Credit Bureau Inc (USA), 53
Credit, computer master files on, 55
Credit Default Register, 157
Credit, purchasing with, 149–59
Credit Rating Agencies, 149–54
Credit-worthiness, security of information on, 146–9
Crime, bugging used to detect, 37–8
Criminal records and subsequent employment, 162–4
Criminal Records Office, 86–93
CUAB, see Cambridge University Appointments Board

Daily Mail, exposing drug traffic by, 193
Dangerous Drugs Act (1970), 84
Data Banks and Centres, 60–2; control of access to, 82–3; of medical histories, 71–4, 187; proposed Tribunal for, 155
Debt recovery, 135, 150, 156–9; methods adopted for, 158–9, 195–6
Defamation, protection of existing law against, 203–6
Detectives, private, 134–7, 141–2; offences by, 199; proposal to license, 145; reprehensible practices by, 143–5
Devices used to breach privacy, 27–32; aural, 35–6; tailing, 37; visual, 34–5

Dissidents, 95
Divorce case enquiries, 135
Douty, Alderman H. H. C., 168–9
Drugs, search of person in pursuit of, 84–5, 166
Dyes and powders, use of, 27

Edelman, Maurice (MP), 188–90, 193 (mentioned), 195
Educational master files on computer, 55; see also Students and privacy.
EJP Publications (James Pike) Ltd, 134
Employment Agencies Federation, 160
Employment, restrictions of, on security grounds, 99–103
Enquiries by employers during job selection, 160; see also Aptitude tests
Entering premises, the right to, 84, 105, 116, 123, 130
Espionage, 97–8, 177

Fees for supplying secret information, 136–7
Fingerprints, 66, 88–90
Fostering cases, Press intrusion into, 130
Franks Report (1973), 23
Freud, Ann, 168–9

Gorst, J. M. (MP), 194
Green, Mrs (cohabitation case), 114
Greene, Sir Hugh, 133
Gross, Martin L., 42–3
Guardian, The, experiment, 137–40, 145 (mentioned)

Harassment when debt recovering, law against, 159
Harber, Julian, 168–9
'Harmonica' bug, 32–3
Harvey, Peter, 137–40, 140–1
Heffer, Eric (MP), 176–8
Henderson, A. E., 103
Hospitals, Press intrusion at, 129
How Green Was My Valley (Richard Llewellyn), 14–15
Huckfield, Leslie (MP), 155–6
Huddleston, Father, 101

IBA, 133
Impersonation, see Personation
Income Tax Management Act (1964), 187
Information: access to computer, 63–5; by computer, distortions in, 65–7
Infra-red light, use of, 28–30, 40
Inland Revenue, computer for, 188
International Commission of Jurists, 58–9
International Labour Office, 47–8
Intrusion, techniques of, 26–40
Investigation and Trade Protection Bureau, 157
Investigator, The, 142
IQ and computers, 69–70

Job-hunting and -suitability, questionnaires on, 159–64
Jones, Mervyn, 122–8
Jones, Mrs (cohabitation case), 112
Jones, R. V., 32–3

Keeler, Christine, 132
Kemps Mercantile Offices, 152

Kentlaun Agencies, 157

Law: information needed for enforcement of, for computer, 60; proposed amendments to, 200–1, 211–20; protection of existing, 203–6
Leadbitter, Ted (MP), 195–6
Leaks from official sources, how private detectives obtain, 137–8
Legislation, proposed to cover right of privacy, 200–1, 211–20
Libel, protection afforded by law of, 203–6
Licences for private detectives, proposal for, 144–5
Lister, Ruth, 110–21
Loyalty, watchdogs of, 95–105
Lyon, Alexander W. (MP), 12, 179, 184, 216–20
Lyttelton, Oliver (MP), 101

McCarthyism, 18
Madgwick, Donald, 37–8, 39–40
Magnetic card files, 56–7
Manaton Central Register of Defaulters, 156
Masquerading, see Personation
Mass media, exposition by, 122–34, 188–9, 193–5
Matusow, Harvey, 74–5
Medical histories, computer storage of, 61, 71–4, 187–8, 190–3
Merken, Peter, 136
Microphones, 31–2, 33–4, 40, 133, 173 (mentioned), 197
Microwave beams, use of, 33–4
Middlemen, the rôle of, in obtaining secret information, 138–9

MI5, 95–6, 100–2
Miller, Arthur R., 41–4, 57, 65–7
Minnesota Multiphasic Test, 48
Minority Report (A. W. Lyon), 216–20
Missing Persons Index, 89–90, 135
Mistakes on computer, 74–5
Mitchell, R. C. (MP), 189–90, 193–5
Money Which?, 147–8
Montgomery, Dr D., 167

National Association of Trade Protection Societies (NATPS), 150
National Council for Civil Liberties, 37–8, 40, 62–5, 68–71, 75–6, 85, 106, 107, 134–7, 156–9, 160
National Federation of Professional Workers, 161
National Union of Students, 164
News of the World, allegations made by, 194
Newspaper publicity, see Mass media, exposition by
1984 (Orwell), 19, 216
Noble, William, 135

Official Secrets Act (1911), 23
Official surveys, 106

Peace Pledge Union, 102
Pen registers, 57
People, The, exposure of bribery by, 193
Personality Tests, 41–4, 44–6, 47–8; see also Reactive assessment

Personation, 142, 143, 199
Personnel, screening of, 60
Peters, Mrs (cohabitation case), 119–20
Petro, Dr John, 193
Pills, radio type, 28
Police: bugging devices used by, 37–8; powers of arrest by, 90; records, 84–94 (see also Computers, use of, for police records); 'stop checks' by, 90–3
Postal services, use of magnetic card files for, 56–7
Press, see Mass media, exposition by
Press Council, 132
Prisoners on release seeking employment, 161–2
Privacy: Bill (1967), 11–12, 172–81; Bill (1970), 206–10; cases where convictions secured when infringing, 199; cases where there is no legal right of, 197–8; Committee on (1972), terms of reference, 11, legislative conclusions summarised, 211–20; definition, 12–15; incursion by State into, 17–20; Minority Report, 216–20; parliamentary debates on (1970), 172–81 (1973), 181–96; proposed law amendments on, 200–1, 206–11, 211–20; respecting students, 164–71; right of, 196–211 and definition of proposed right of, 210; tort of, advocated, 216–20; White Paper on, proposed, 186
Private detectives, see Detectives, private
Psychiatrists' use of computers, 68–71, 191

Psychological tests, 41–4, 44–6, 47–8
Publicity, see Mass media, exposition by
Public mischief, 140–1
Public servants, information received indirectly by, 105–21

Quartermaine, Barry, 136

Race Relations Act, 159
Radio, see Mass media, exposition by
Radio transmitters, 27, 143
Raison, Timothy (MP), 190–3
Reactive assessment, 49–51
Read, David, 136–7
Real time computing, 63
Recording techniques, use of surreptitious, 132–3
Reprehensible practices (by private detectives), 143–5
Retail Credit Company (USA), 53
Rex, John, 100–1
Right of Privacy Act (1970), proposed, 206–10
Rolph, C. H., 38
Rorschach ink-blot test, 48
Rule, James B., 86–95, 162–4

Sawyer with Schechter, 62
Schools Action Union, London, 168
Search, power of and right to, 84, 116
Security risks of the State, 97–8, 100–5
Security Services, private, 135
Security systems safeguarding computerised information, 75–6, 77

Shepherd, Christina, 104–5
Soames, Sir Christopher, 102
Social Security Benefits, 108–21
Sohn, Louis B., 33
Special Branch activities, 95–105, *passim*
Spike Mikes, 33–4
Spying, 97–8, 177
Statistical records of students, 164–5
Statistics of Trade Act (1947), 106
Status Investigators Ltd, 157
Status reporting, 153–4; *see also* Bankers' references
Stein, Mrs, 99
'Stop checks' by police, 90–3
Students and privacy, 164–71
Supplementary Benefits Commission, 108–21

Tagging Transmitters, 27–8
Tape recorders, 31, 133
Techniques of intrusion, 26–40
Telephones, access by, to computer data banks, 63–4; devices affecting, 32–3, 40, 57; tapping of, 95, 135 (mentioned)
Telephoto lenses, 30, 133, 193, 197
Television, closed circuit, 29; *see also* Mass media, exposition by
Times, The, example of investigative journalism by, 189–90
Tournier v National Provincial and Union Bank of England, 148
Tort of privacy, advocated, 216–20
Trades Union Congress, 160–1
Transmitters, miniaturised, 33

Trespass, 123, 143, 173

UAPT, *see* United Association for the Protection of Trade
UCCA, *see* Universities Central Council on Admissions
United Association for the Protection of Trade, 150–4
Universities Central Council on Admissions, 164–5
University of East Anglia, 166–7

Vehicle licensing by computer, 187

Walden, Brian (MP), 11–12, 172–6, 206–10
Walker, Peter (MP), 107
Wanted Persons Index, 89–90
Warren, Mr and Mrs Samuel D., 201–6
Warwick University, 167–71
Watkins, Alan, 177
Westin, Professor Alan F., 27–32, 38–9, 44–6, 47–8, 51 (mentioned), 53–6, 60–1, 62 (mentioned)
White, Mrs (cohabitation case), 113
Williams, Shirley (MP), 187
Wireless Telegraphy Act (1949), 143, 199
Withers, Ian, 140–1
Wives, vetting employees', 136
Wolf, Michael, 170–1

Younger, Sir Kenneth, 12
Younger Report, *passim*: *but see also* Privacy *under* Committee on (1972)

M4